# Business Valuation Management – Corporate Valuation

**Dr. P.K. Bandgar**
*M.Com., Ph.D., FICWA,*
Director, Oriental Institute of Management,
Sector 12, Vashi,
Navi Mumbai - 400703.

MUMBAI • NEW DELHI • NAGPUR • BENGALURU • HYDERABAD • CHENNAI • PUNE • LUCKNOW • AHMEDABAD • ERNAKULAM • BHUBANESWAR • INDORE • KOLKATA • GUWAHATI

**First Edition : 2014**

---

**Published by** : Mrs. Meena Pandey for **Himalaya Publishing House Pvt. Ltd.,**
"Ramdoot", Dr. Bhalerao Marg, Girgaon, **Mumbai - 400 004.**
Phone: 022-23860170/23863863, Fax: 022-23877178
**E-mail: himpub@vsnl.com; Website: www.himpub.com**

**Branch Offices** :

**New Delhi** : "Pooja Apartments", 4-B, Murari Lal Street, Ansari Road, Darya Ganj, New Delhi - 110 002. Phone: 011-23270392, 23278631; Fax: 011-23256286

**Nagpur** : Kundanlal Chandak Industrial Estate, Ghat Road, Nagpur - 440 018. Phone: 0712-2738731, 3296733; Telefax: 0712-2721216

**Bengaluru** : No. 16/1 (Old 12/1), 1st Floor, Next to Hotel Highlands, Madhava Nagar, Race Course Road, Bengaluru - 560 001. Phone: 080-22286611, 22385461, 4113 8821, 22281541

**Hyderabad** : No. 3-4-184, Lingampally, Besides Raghavendra Swamy Matham, Kachiguda, Hyderabad - 500 027. Phone: 040-27560041, 27550139

**Chennai** : 8/2 Madley 2nd street, T. Nagar, Chennai - 600 017. Mobile: 09320490962

**Pune** : First Floor, "Laksha" Apartment, No. 527, Mehunpura, Shaniwarpeth (Near Prabhat Theatre), Pune - 411 030. Phone: 020-24496323/24496333; Mobile: 09370579333

**Lucknow** : House No 731, Shekhupura Colony, Near B.D. Convent School, Aliganj, Lucknow - 226 022. Mobile: 09307501549

**Ahmedabad** : 114, "SHAIL", 1st Floor, Opp. Madhu Sudan House, C.G. Road, Navrang Pura, Ahmedabad - 380 009. Phone: 079-26560126; Mobile: 09377088847

**Ernakulam** : 39/176 (New No: 60/251) 1st Floor, Karikkamuri Road, Ernakulam, Kochi – 682011. Phone: 0484-2378012, 2378016; Mobile: 09387122121

**Bhubaneswar** : 5 Station Square, Bhubaneswar - 751 001 (Odisha). Phone: 0674-2532129, Mobile: 09338746007

**Indore** : Kesardeep Avenue Extension, 73, Narayan Bagh, Flat No. 302, IIIrd Floor, Near Humpty Dumpty School, Indore - 452 007 (M.P.). Mobile: 09303399304

**Kolkata** : 108/4, Beliaghata Main Road, Near ID Hospital, Opp. SBI Bank, Kolkata - 700 010, Phone: 033-32449649, Mobile: 7439040301

**Guwahati** : House No. 15, Behind Pragjyotish College, Near Sharma Printing Press, P.O. Bharalumukh, Guwahati - 781009, (Assam). Mobile: 09883055590, 08486355289, 7439040301

**DTP by** : Pravin Kharche

**Printed at** : Geetanjali Press Pvt. Ltd. Nagpur. On behalf of HPH.

# Preface

It is a matter of great privilege for me to place before the esteemed readers the first edition of the book **"Business Valuation Management – Corporate Valuation"**. Changes in business management have profoundly affected cost accounting and cost management at the beginning of the twenty-first century. These changes are an increased emphasis on providing value to customers, globalization of markets, growth of service, industry and awareness of ethical and environmental business practices. Therefore, the new value management system can be more accurately referred to as an activity and strategic management system.

This book covers lucid presentation, tailor-made approach, comprehensive text with plenty of illustrations and has several additional welcome features. The book covers the course contents of the students appearing for MBA/MMS of the University of Mumbai and other universities in India and CA, CS and ICAI and other professional examinations. I am confident that with all these features, the students and faculties will find this book all the more useful and rewarding. This book is dedicated to Lord Ganesha who is a constant source of energy and involvement in serving the students and teacher-community. Constructive and helpful suggestions for improvement of this book will be gratefully acknowledged.

I am very much thankful to Dr. M.G. Shirahtti, Directer General, Oriental Institute of Management, Vashi, Navi Mumbai for his inspiration and support while writing this book.

I am very much thankful to Mr. S.K. Srivastava, Mr. S.K. Patil, Nimisha Kadam and all staff members of Himalaya Publishing House Pvt. Ltd., Nahur, Mumbai for their personal involvement in the publication of the book.

**Dr. P.K. Bandgar**

# Table of Contents


| Sr. No. | Title | Page No. |
|---|---|---|
| 1 | Business Valuation | 1 - 14 |
| 2 | Approaches to Valuation | 15 - 38 |
| 3 | Discounted Cash Flow Valuation | 39 - 55 |
| 4 | Relative Valuation | 56 - 77 |
| 5 | Brand Valuations | 78 - 89 |
| 6 | Valuing Private Companies | 90 - 107 |
| 7 | Option Pricing Application in Valuation | 108 - 118 |
| 8 | Valuation in Acquisitions | 119 - 139 |
| 9 | Value Enhancement | 140 - 168 |

# Chapter 1 BUSINESS VALUATION

1.1 Introduction
1.2 Definition of Value and Valuation
1.3 Need for Valuation
1.4 Valuation Concepts
1.5 Corporate Form of Organisation
1.6 Raising Capital by Corporates
1.7 Corporate Valuation
1.8 Exercises

## 1.1 INTRODUCTION

A business valuation is a complex process and it involves a multitude of factors ranging from financial matters to historical perspectives. It is a broad and technically challenging discipline. The valuation is performed in a variety of contexts and for a variety of purposes. The word 'value' means different things to different people, and the result will not be the same should the context change. A valuation is not an exact science. Value is a subjective term and can have a different connotation. Valuation involves use of professional judgement, knowledge of business, analysis of facts, interpretations, and usage of different methods and procedures, which may result into different values in each given situation. During the last decade, several changes have taken place in economic and business environment. The pace of growth has been phenomenal. The continuity in growth of business and emergence of the new generation entrepreneur, has tremendously increased participation of the public in the financial market, and development of new financial markets. All these have led to a greater demand for valuation services, as investors and shareholders are interested in up to date information on their assets. The valuation is considered as heart of finance. In corporate finance, it is required to consider, how best to increase firm value by changing its investment, financing and dividend decisions. In portfolio management, the resources are extended, trying to find firms that trade of less than their true value, and then hope to generate profits as price coverage on value.

## 1.2 DEFINITION OF VALUE AND VALUATION

The word 'value' in simple terms refers to intrinsic worth of an object or a thing. A thing which is valuable is expected to possess utility. Thus, anything which has utility will have same worth or value. Value, is a subjective term and may differ from person to person, from place to place, from time to time, and from one situation to another. Thus, value is mere subjective perception. There is always a subjective connotation associated with value and valuation.

Valuation refers to the process of assessing value or price. Valuation is the process of estimating what something is worth. Business valuation is the process of determining the current worth of a business by use of objective measures and offer evaluation of all aspects of business. Items that call for valuation are mostly financial assets or liabilities. It is very common to value assets or liabilities. For example, investments in marketable securities, stocks, options, business enterprise or intangibles like goodwill, patents, trademarks, copyrights. Valuation of business may be required for a variety of reasons such as investment analysis, long-term investment decisions, capital budgeting, mergers and acquisitions, demergers, dividend decisions, share buybacks, litigations, tax related valuations including transfer pricing. The importance of business valuation has assumed great significance in recent times in the wake of economic liberalization, where controls began to pave the way for deregulation, and corporate acquisitions and mergers have become the order of the day. Business valuation, to be effective should be clearly defined and the objectives sought should be achieved to be properly ascertained. It is imperative to take into consideration, factors like the nature and history of the business, the present financial status of the business, the general economic conditions prevailing in the company and also the industry in which the company operates.

## 1.3 NEED FOR VALUATION

Valuation is used by financial market participants to determine the price, they are willing to pay or receive to consummate a sale of business. The need for valuing a business or a firm can well be identified by various purposes. The purposes, that a valuation serves are manifold. A valuation may be used for a wide range of purposes. These purposes are as follows:

1. Mergers and Acquisitions
2. Takeovers
3. Demergers
4. Sales/Disinvestments
5. Public issue of shares
6. Pledge of shares
7. To settle taxation disputes
8. To decide the partner's share

From the buyer's point of view the valuation tells him the price he should pay. From the seller's point of view, the valuation will tell him the lowest price at which he should be prepared to sell. In case of a listed company, valuation is useful to compare the value obtained with the share price on the stock exchange, and to decide whether to sell or buy or hold the shares. Valuation of several companies may be useful to make portfolio decisions. When the shares are offered to the public, the valuation is used to justify the price at which the shares are offered to the public.

Valuation of a company provides a fundamental benchmark to identify and satisfy the main value drivers. It is a prior step in making strategic decisions such as to continue business, sell, merge, grow or acquire other companies. In the case of strategic planning, the valuation of the company and different business units are fundamental for deciding what products, business lines, countries and customers to maintain, grow or abandon. It also provides means for measuring the impact of the company's possible policies and strategies on value creation and destruction.

## 1.4 VALUATION CONCEPTS

The term 'valuation' means the task of estimating the worth of an asset, a security or a business. The price an investor or a firm is willing to purchase a specific asset or security would be related to this valuation. Obviously, two different buyers may not have the same valuation of a business, as their perception regarding its worth may vary. One may perceive the business to be of higher worth, and hence may be willing to pay a higher price than the other. A seller would consider the negotiated selling price of the business to be greater than the value of business he is selling.

There are subjective considerations involved in the task and process of valuation. The task of business valuation is more important than that of an asset. In case of business valuation, the valuation is required not only of tangible assets, but also of intangible assets like goodwill, brands, patents and trademarks. It also requires to value human resources that manage the business. There is an imperative need to take into consideration, recorded liabilities as well as unrecorded or contingent liabilities, so that the buyer is aware of the total sum payable subsequent to the purchase of business. That is why, the valuation process is affected by subjective considerations. Thus, in order to reduce the element of subjectivity, and help the finance manager to carry out a more credible valuation exercise in an objective manner, the following concepts of valuation needs to be understood.

(i) **Book value:** Book value of business is the total value of all valuable assets, less all external liabilities including preference share capital. It is also known as net assets value or net worth of business.

(ii) **Market value:** The market value of business is the aggregate market price of all equity shares outstanding of the company. The market value is the price of company's share quoted in the stock market. It is applicable to a company whose shares are listed in the stock exchange.

(iii) **Economic value:** The economic value indicates the maximum price at which the business can be acquired. Economic value is the present value of incremental future cash inflows using an appropriate discount rate. The principle of valuation based on the discounted cash flow approach is used in capital budgeting decisions. It is an economic value.

(iv) **Intrinsic value:** Intrinsic value is based on the net assets of the firm. It is based on book value, which is in tune with the going concern principle of accounting. For this purpose, it is assumed that the company goes into liquidation and therefore, the tangible and intangible assets are valued satisfactorily, and the total external liabilities are deducted from the value of realisable assets. The net asset value is divided by the number of equity shares to arrive at intrinsic value per share.

(v) **Liquidation value:** Liquidation value represents the price at which each individual asset can be sold, if business operations are discontinued in the wake of liquidation of the firm. Thus, the liquidation value of a business is equal to the sum of realisable value of assets and cash in bank, less the payments required to discharge all external liabilities.

(vi) **Replacement value:** The replacement value is the cost of acquiring a new asset of equal utility usefulness. It is normally useful in valuing tangible assets like machinery, equipment and furniture. These assets have a useful life but they can be replaced with new assets before the expiry of their life.

(vii) **Salvage value:** Salvage value represents realisable scrap value on the disposal of assets after the expiry of their useful economic life. It can be used to value assets like plant and machinery, equipment and furniture. The salvage value is considered net of removal costs.

(viii) **Fair value:** Fair value is the average of book value and market value of shares. It is hybrid in nature, and often, the average of two or three values. In India, the concept of fair value has evolved from case laws, and is applicable to certain specific transactions like payment to minority shareholders.

## 1.5 CORPORATE FORM OF ORGANISATION

Corporate means a company. A company is an important form of business organisation. A company is registered as per the Companies Act, 1956. A company is a voluntary association of persons formed for the purpose of carrying on business. The capital is contributed by the members, and the profit is also shared by the members. The company form of organisation has grown tremendously, particularly, after globalisation in 1991. There are more than twelve lakhs of companies functioning in India, the breakup of which is given below:

| | |
|---|---|
| No. of Companies registered | 12,89,229 |
| No. of Private Ltd. Companies | 11,67,226 |
| No. of Public Ltd. Companies | 1,22,003 |
| No. of Active Companies | 8,72,957 |
| No. of Inactive Companies | 4,16,272 |

***Source:*** Corporate Affairs Ministry, 2012.

The company form of organisation has become popular because of the following features:

(i) **Large capital:** A company can raise large amount of capital by issue of shares to the public, which is not possible for any other form of business organisation.

(ii) **Transfer of shares:** Shares issued by the companies are transferable from person to person. The stock exchanges are formed for this purpose. The shares are traded on the stock exchanges. Shareholders can sell or buy the shares through the stock market. This facility is not there in case of other business organisations.

(iii) **Limited liability:** The liability of a member of a company is limited to the extent of his shareholding. However, the liability of a sole trader or a partner in the firm is unlimited.

(iv) **Separation of ownership from management:** In case of a company form of an organisation, the shareholders are the owners and the Board of Directors is the management. The day to day business decisions are taken by the Board of Directors, but the shareholders are not involved in the day to day matters of the business.

Basically there are two types of companies, Private Limited and Public Limited. Private Limited company is a company, which (a) restricts number of members to 50 (b) restricts transfer of shares and (c) is prohibited from issuing of prospectus for issue of shares to the public. Public Limited company is a company which is not a Private Limited company. To form a private limited company, minimum two persons are required whereas, to form a public limited company, minimum seven persons are required. The minimum number of persons, who are involved in the formation of the company are called 'Promoters'. A private limited company can start business immediately after registration, but a public limited company has to obtain a Certificate of Commencement of Business from the Registrar of Companies. The promoters of private limited company can raise capital by issue of shares to their friends and relatives because the number of members should not go beyond 50. The basic condition for getting the Certificate of Commencement of Business is collection of minimum subscription of share capital. At the time of registration of a company, the promoters have to submit two important documents i.e. (a) Memorandum of Association and (b) Articles of Association.

The Memorandum of Association is the constitution of the company, which includes:

(i) Name of the company
(ii) Registered address
(iii) Objects of the company
(iv) Share capital
(v) Liability

The Articles of the Association contains the internal rules and regulations for the day to day working of the company.

## 1.6 RAISING CAPITAL BY CORPORATES

Public limited companies can raise capital by issue of shares, debentures or bonds to the public. The amount of capital to be raised, and the sources of capital are to be decided by the Board of Directors. It is also guided by the Memorandum of Association. However, the companies can raise capital by issue of the following instruments:

### (1) Equity Shares

**Share** means a share in the share capital of a company. A company is a business organization. It is registered as per Companies Act, 1956. Every company has share capital. The share capital of a company is divided into number of equal parts and each of such part is known as a 'share'. A public limited company has to complete three stages. The first is registration. The second is raising capital and the third is commencement of business. A public limited company issues shares to the public for raising capital. The first public issue is known as **Initial Public Offerings (IPO)**. The shares can be issued at par, premium or discount. Each share has a face value of ₹ 1, 2, 5 or 10. In order to issue shares a prospectus is prepared, and has to be approved by the Securities and Exchange Board of India (SEBI). These shares are listed with the stock exchange, so that the shareholders can sell these shares in the market. The company has to make an application to the stock exchange for listing of shares.

There are two types of shares, equity shares and preference shares. Preference shares are those shares, which have first preference for payment of dividend and refund of capital, in case of winding up. Equity shares are those shares, which are not preference shares. Preference shares are not popular in India. Very few companies have issued preference shares. The preference shares may be cumulative, participating and convertible. The shares are also called as **"stock"**. Nowadays, shares are issued in Demat form. It means, shares are credited to a separate account of the applicant, opened with depository participant. This is also called paperless security, because shares are not issued in physical form. Demat account is compulsory, when the shares are issued through Book Building Process. Book Building is a method of public issue of shares by a company in which, the price is determined by the investors, subject to a price band or range of prices given by the company.

**Blue Chip Shares: Shares of known and financially sound companies are called blue chip shares.** Such companies are called **blue chip companies,** as they are well established over a long period and are stable and profitable. Such companies have a record of consistent growth over years and have bright future. Blue chip companies are popular in the stock market and **they carry goodwill and market reputation**. Such companies are managed by professionals and offer attractive dividend to shareholders. Blue chip shares have continuous market demand as **investors prefer to invest in blue chip companies due to safety, security and attractive return**. Even when the stock market is dull, the prices of blue chip shares do not go down quickly and considerably. In India, **Reliance, Tata Companies, L&T and companies relating to information technology are regarded as blue chip companies**. Their shares are quoted at higher prices in the stock market. Bank gives loan easily and quickly on the security of blue chip shares.

Investment in shares is more risky, because the share prices go on changing day by day. Today, the market is more **'volatile',** means more fluctuating. The share prices may go up or go down. If the stock market falls, the share prices will go down, and the investor will loose money in the investment. However, the return on investment in shares is higher. The return on investment in shares is in the form of regular dividend, capital appreciation, bonus and rights. There is also liquidity in this kind of investment. The shares can be sold in stock market and money can be collected within 3 to 4 days. Investment in shares is not a tax saving investment.

Joint stock companies collect their long term/fixed capital by issuing shares (equity and preference). This is called **"stock financing"**. Shares constitute the ownership securities and are popular among the investing class. **Investment in shares is risky as well as profitable.** Transactions in shares take place in the primary and secondary markets. Large majority of investors (particularly small investors) prefer to purchase shares through brokers and other dealers operating on commission basis. Purchasing of shares is now easy and quick due to the extensive use of computers and screen based trading system (SBTs). Orders can be registered on computers. The shares available for investment are classified into different categories such as **blue chip shares, growth shares, speculative shares, income shares and so on**. For profitable investment in shares, the companies must be selected properly by studying the balance sheets and other details of various companies. Share certificates in physical form are no more popular in India due to **demat facility**. It gives convenience in handling and transfer of shares. For this, demat account can be opened in the bank which provides depository services (e.g., ICICI Demat).

### Advantages of Investment in Shares

1. **Equity shareholders get income in the form of dividend.** Companies offer attractive dividend to shareholders even when the rate of dividend is flexible. Profitable and stable companies offer good reward to their investors in the form of high rate of dividend.
2. **The liability of equity shareholders is limited** only to the extent of their investment. Naturally, the shareholder is not required to pay anything more than the face value of the shares purchased.
3. **Shares are easily transferable and** this facilitates easy transfer of ownership at the option of shareholder (i.e., investor). This transfer facility (transferability) also brings **liquidity** to the investment in shares.
4. The equity shareholders get an **opportunity to participate in the profitability of their company** in the course of time. The profitable company **issues bonus shares** and also **right**

**shares** from time to time. This gives benefit to shareholders. Even the new shares issued by the company are first offered to existing shareholders. This **pre-emptive right** enables existing shareholders to maintain their proportional ownership in the additional equity share capital issued.

5. Listed equity shares are actively quoted and traded on stock exchanges. This **marketability of equity shares brings liquidity to the investment in** shares and also convenience to investors.
6. Equity shares carry **tax benefit**. At present dividend on shares of Indian companies has been made tax-free. However the position may change as per the government policy.
7. **Equity shareholders are the owners of their company with certain powers and voting rights.** This enables them (collectively) **to exercise some control** over the policies of their company.
8. **Capital gain to the equity investor is possible** in the case of shares, as the prices of shares fluctuate along with the future prospects of the company. Due to rise in the share prices, there is **capital appreciation** and this offers extra benefit to the shareholders.

**Limitations of Investment in Shares**

1. **Uncertainty of income/return: The return as regards investment in shares is uncertain** as it is linked with the profitability of the company. The investment in shares may prove to be unremunerative, if the profit earned by the company is less.
2. **Risky investment:** In the case of shares, there is **an element of risk as regards changing market values**. The share price may go down due to various reasons. This is bound to affect the investor seriously. **Secondly**, selling at a low price is bound to bring financial loss. This suggests that **investment in shares is always risky**.
3. **Speculative activities are harmful: Speculative activities** are quite common as regards shares. However, such speculative deals affect genuine investors and they may suffer loss even when they are not directly involved in such speculative activities.
4. **Future linked with the company:** In the case of shares, **the future of the shareholder is linked with the future of the company**. The return on investment will be attractive, if the company makes good profit. However, a shareholder may not get any return on his investment if his company fails to get reasonably high profit.

## (2) Preference Shares

As the name indicates, preference shares carry preferential rights as regards dividend payment and repayment of capital in the case of liquidation of the issuing company. Different types of preference shares can be issued. This gives wider choice to investors and raises marketability of preference shares.

**Preference shares offer various advantages to the shareholders.** Here, dividend payment is regular and also at a fixed rate decided at the time of issue. They also get preference as regards repayment of capital, in the case of winding up of the company. **For the company**, the cost of collection of preference capital is low and the redemption liability is nil in the case of irredeemable preference shares.

**Preference Shares have following limitations:-**

1. Preference shareholders have no control on the management of the company.
2. They get dividend at fixed rate and are normally not allowed to be partners in the prosperity of the company.

## Types of Preference Shares

There are different types of preference shares which are as follows:

1. **Cumulative preference shares:** Cumulative preference shares are those preference shares which carry the right to a fixed amount of dividend at a fixed rate. Dividend is payable even out of future profit, if current year's profit is not sufficient for this purpose. This means that dividend on the cumulative preference shares accumulates unless it is paid in full. The arrears of dividend are then shown in the balance sheet as a contingent liability. In India, preference shares are normally cumulative unless otherwise stated. In case the preference dividend is in arrears for a period not less that two years, the preference shareholders shall be entitled to take part and vote on every resolution on every matter in the general meeting of the shareholders.
2. **Non-cumulative preference shares:** Non-cumulative preference shares carry the right to a fixed amount of dividend. In case no dividend is declared in a year due to any reason, the right to receive such dividend for that year expires. It means that, holders of non-cumulative preference shares are not entitled to arrears of dividend in future. If the dividend remains in arrears for a period, not less than two years or an aggregate period of not less than three years, comprised in the six years ending with the expiry of the financial year, the holders of such shares are entitled to take part and vote on every resolution at any meeting of the shareholders.
3. **Participating preference shares:** In addition to the right to a fixed dividend, participating preference shareholders have the right to participate in the surplus profits, after payment of equity dividend at a stipulated rate. Again, in an event of winding up of the company, participating preference shareholders carry the right to receive a pre-determined proportion of surplus as well, once the equity shareholders have been paid off.
4. **Non-participating preference shares:** Non-participating preference shares are the shares on which only a fixed rate of dividend is paid every year, without any additional rights in profits and in the surplus, in case of winding up. Unless otherwise, specified, the preference shares are generally non-participating.
5. **Redeemable preference shares:** Under section 80 of the Companies Act, 1956, a company can issue redeemable preference shares. Redeemable preference shares are issued on the condition that, the company will repay after the fixed period or even earlier, at company's discretion. The repayment of these shares is called redemption of preference shares. In India, companies can issue only redeemable preference shares.
6. **Non-redeemable preference shares:** The preference shares, which do not carry with them the arrangement regarding redemption at a certain period, are called non-redeemable preference shares or irredeemable preference shares. Section 80 (5A) provides that no company limited by shares shall issue irredeemable preference shares or preference shares redeemable after the expiry of 20 years from the date of issue.
7. **Convertible preference shares:** Those preference shares give the right to the holder to get them converted into equity shares at their option according to the terms and conditions of their issue are known as convertible preference shares. Preference shares are non-convertible unless otherwise stated.
8. **Non-convertible preference shares:** When the holder of a preference share has not been conferred the right to get his preference shares converted into equity shares is called as non-convertible preference shares. Preference shares are non-convertible unless otherwise stated.

## (3) Bonds or Debentures

A **debenture** is a document issued by a company as an evidence of a debt. It is a certificate issued by a company under its seal, acknowledging a debt due by it to its holders. The term debenture includes debenture stock, bonds and any other securities issued by a company. The Companies Act provides that a company can raise loans from the public by issue of debentures. The debenture holder becomes the creditor of the company. The debenture holder gets interest on the debenture which is fixed at the time of issue. The debentures are also issued to the public just like issue of shares. However, there is a need for credit rating before issue of debentures or bonds. Bonds are issued by Government companies and the debentures are issued by the Private sector companies. Therefore, bonds may be tax saving but debentures are not tax saving investment.

The companies use owned capital as well as borrowed capital in their capital structure as compared to equity shares because debenture holders have no say in the management of the company and interest on debentures is allowed as a business expense for tax purposes. The debentures are considered as secured loan. There is not much risk in the investment in debentures as compared to shares. The return on debentures is also reasonable and stable. The debentures are also listed with the stock exchanges and can be traded in the stock market. However, the prices of debentures are not much volatile.

The debenture, being a loan, is redeemable at a certain period or maturity, otherwise it can be irredeemable. The debentures can be convertible or non-convertible. If a debenture is convertible into shares at maturity, it is called convertible. The convertible debentures may be partly convertible or fully convertible. Convertible debentures became popular in the last decade. The method of raising long-term funds through debentures is not very popular in India. Very few companies have issued debentures and very few companies' debentures or bonds are traded in the stock market. The debentures were also not popular till recent years.

There are different types of debentures which are as follows:

1. **Secured or unsecured debentures:** The debentures which are secured against the assets of the company are known as secured debentures. These debentures are secured by a charge upon some or all the assets of the company. There are two types of charges, fixed charge and floating charge. A fixed charge is a mortgage on specific assets of the company. These assets cannot be sold or transferred without the consent of the debenture holder. The sale proceeds of these secured assets are utilised first for repaying debentures. A floating charge generally covers all the assets of the company including future assets.

   The debentures which are not secured by any charge upon any assets of the company are called as unsecured debentures. Sometimes these debentures are also called as 'naked' debentures. A company merely promises to pay interest on due dates and repay the amount of debentures at maturity. These types of debentures are very risky. In India, debentures are normally secured against the assets of the Company.

2. **Convertible or non-convertible debentures:** The debentures which can be converted into equity shares after a certain time are known as convertible debentures. These debentures may be converted at par or at premium or even at discount. There may be fully convertible debentures or partly convertible debentures. Fully convertible debentures means, full amount of debenture is convertible into shares. On the other hand, partly convertible debentures means a certain portion of debenture amount is converted into shares and remaining portion is repaid to the debentureholder at maturity. Thus, convertible debentures have become

popular because the debentureholders get the chance to become the shareholder of the company. A new concept of debentures has been developed recently known as 'Optionally Fully Convertible Debentures' (OFCD). In case of these debentures, the conversion takes place at the option of the debenture holder at the time of maturity. The market price of the company's share may change at the time of conversion if the price of the shares has increased, otherwise the debentureholder may opt for redemption at maturity.

Non-convertible debentures are those which cannot be converted into shares at maturity. The debentureholders will get cash at maturity as per terms of issue.

3. **Redeemable or irredeemable debentures:** The debentures which are redeemed at a certain period of maturity are known as Redeemable debentures. The debentures are redeemable as per terms of the issue. The maturity period is fixed at the time of issue of debentures. It may be six months or 7 years, as the case may be. Since debenture is a kind of loan taken by the company from the public, it has to be repaid after some time. The management of the company decides the maturity period on the basis of their financial plans.

   The debentures, which are not repayable during the lifetime of the company are called as irredeemable debentures. These are also called as 'perpetual debentures.' These debentures are repaid only at the time of liquidation of the company. Normally, in India, the debentures are redeemable at a certain time.

4. **Registered and Bearer debentures:** Registered debentures are payable to a registered holder whose name, address, and other particulars of holding are recorded in the Register of debenture holders by the company. These are not easily transferable. However, the necessary provisions of the Companies Act, 1956 are to be complied with, for affecting transfer of these debentures. The debenture interest is paid by the company, to the order of registered holder as expressed in the warrant issued by the company. In India, debentures are normally registered.

   The debentures issued by the company, without keeping any record in respect of their holders are called 'Bearer Debentures.' These debentures are transferable by delivery. These debentures are negotiable instruments payable to the bearer. Debenture interest is paid to the bearer of the interest coupons or the debenture holder at the time of payment of interest. Such types of debentures are normally not issued in India.

## Features of Debentures

Debentures are issued for raising short, medium or long-term finance depending on the period for which they are issued. Debentures are **creditorship securities,** which provide funds on loan basis. Debenture holders are not allowed to participate in the management of the company, as they are the **creditors of** the company and not the **owners**. However, they are given more security as regards repayment of capital and regular payment of interest.

Different types of debentures are issued on different terms and conditions in order to satisfy the needs of different categories of investors. The book value of debentures is usually ₹ 100. At present, debentures (particularly convertible) are popular. Such debentures are converted into equity shares (partly or fully) on maturity, as per the terms already notified.

## Interest on Debentures

The interest rate on all types of debentures is **stable and attractive to investors**. It is paid after every six months or in lump sum on maturity. The risk involved in the purchase of debentures is limited, as they are usually fully secured. The response from investors is always encouraging for the companies issuing debentures. Debentures occupy an important position in the financial structure of companies. Convertible debentures are popular in Indian securities market.

**Advantages of Debentures**

1. Debentures are **popular with the investors** and their response is normally positive.
2. Debentures **provide capital without managerial control** to the debenture holders.
3. It is an **economical** source of finance.
4. Debentures **facilitate trading on equity** by the company.
5. Debentures **avoid the possibility of overcapitalisation**.
6. Debentures **provide adequate safety to investors** particularly to cautious investors.

In addition to company deposits, it is possible to purchase bonds and debentures of joint stock companies for investment purpose. Both represent **creditorship securities**. Debenture indicates loan given to the company at a specific rate of interest and on certain terms and conditions. Debentures are more popular than shares due to the safety and security available. Companies issue different types of debentures for the convenience of investors. At present, **convertible bonds and debentures** are popular among Indian investors.

In India, bonds and debentures are also issued by public sector companies and financial institutions. **IDBI issues flexibonds, deep discount bonds, retirement bonds, growing interest bonds and regular income bonds.** Such **infrastructure** bonds are popular among the investors and their response is encouraging. They are oversubscribed on many occasions. This is particularly due to tax benefit u/s 88. **Deep discount bonds are issued for a longer period** (15 years or more) and investor gets attractive return, if he is willing to wait for a longer period. In April, 1996 **Krishna Bhagyajala Nigam** issued 17.50% non-convertible bonds. It may be noted that **deep discount bonds** offer special benéfits to investors who are willing to invest for a longer period. The interest rate is attractive and the cumulative benefit is available to bond holders. The risk involved is limited, provided the bond issuing institution is reputed and professionally managed. For example, **Sardar Sarovar Narmada Nigam Limited** (Gujarat) issued deep discount bonds in 1995 at a discounted price of ₹ 3,600. On maturity, i.e., in January 2014, the bond holders will get ₹ 1,11,000 as maturity price. Here, ₹ 3,600 will be converted into ₹ 1,11,000 after a period of 20 years.

In addition, in March, 1996, **the Indian Railway Finance Corporation Ltd**. issued **IRFC** secured non-convertible 16.5% bonds of ₹ 50,00,000. The bonds issued include regular return bonds, cumulative bonds and deep discount bonds. Public sector bonds normally get good response from the investing class. **This popularity is due to the following advantages available:**

1. Easy transferability by endorsement and delivery.
2. Safety and security due to government backing.
3. Attractive interest and other favourable terms and conditions, including wide choice as regards selection of bonds.
4. Investment exempted for wealth tax.
5. Maturity period from 5 years to 25 years.
6. Listing on nearby stock exchange.
7. Simple procedure for investment.

**Government of India Savings Bonds**

1. **Government of India 8.0% Savings (taxable) Bonds:**

   The GOI has recently introduced this 8% savings (taxable) bonds. These bonds are convenient for charitable trusts. It is the best option for investment of surplus funds. There is no maximum limit for investment in the bonds. 8% interest payable is taxable.

   **Important features of 8.0% Savings (taxable) Bonds:**

   (a) **Who can buy:** Resident Individuals (not NRI), Minor, HUF, Charitable Institutions and Universities.

   (b) **Interest:** 8.0% p.a., payable half yearly or ₹ 1,000 becomes ₹ 1,601 after 6 years. Half yearly or cumulative interest payment options available. Interest is eligible for deduction u/s 80L (upto ₹ 15,000).

   (c) **Period:** 6 years.

   (d) **Investment:** Any amount, i.e., no limit on the amount of investment.

   (e) **Tax benefit:** Interest is taxable but wealth tax exempted.

   (f) **Transferability:** Bonds are not transferable and pledgable.

   (g) **No TDS will be deducted** on interest.

   (h) **Nomination facility is available.**

   The NRIs are not allowed to invest their funds in these savings bonds.

2. **9.00% GOI Senior Citizens Savings Scheme:**

   It is a special investment scheme introduced for the benefit of senior citizens. It gives attractive return to senior citizens and is popular among them.

   **Important features of 9.00% GOI Senior Citizens Savings Scheme:**

   (a) Resident Indians aged 60 years and above can invest in this scheme.

   (b) Interest rate is 9%, and is payable quarterly.

   (c) Period of scheme is 5 years.

   (d) Ceiling for maximum permissible deposit per person is ₹ 15 lac.

   (e) Account can be opened jointly with spouse only.

   (f) No TDS will be deducted but interest taxable.

   (g) Premature withdrawal facility is available after one year.

   (h) Nomination facility is available.

3. **Government of India 6.50% Savings (Tax free) Bonds:**

   Recently, the government has started issuing 6.50% (Tax free) bonds which are reasonably attractive and secured investment for individuals and institutions.

   **Important features of 6.50% Savings (Tax free) Bonds:**

   (a) Resident individuals (not NRI), HUF and minor through guardian can invest in these bonds.

   (b) No maximum limit on the amount of investment in these bonds.

   (c) Interest 6.50%. Interest payable half yearly or cumulative. Interest payment is exempted from income tax – No wealth tax.

   (d) Maturity period is of **five years.**

(e) Pledge and transfer are not allowed. However, the bonds can be transferable only by way of gifts.

(f) Cumulative facility available. ₹ 1,000 becomes ₹ 1,377 after five years.

(g) Non-cumulative facility is also available. This means 6.5% interest p.a. (payable half yearly). This 6.50% tax free interest is equal to 9.28 p.a. taxable (for 30.0% tax payer).

(h) Redemption (premature encashment) is allowed after 3 years only.

(i) Nomination facility is available.

It may be noted that 6.50% savings bonds offers more benefits/concessions as compared to 8% savings (taxable) bonds. Both the bonds are popular and used extensively as a safe and secured investment avenue by large number of rich investors. **Both the avenues are not available to NRIs.** The new Savings Bonds of GOI are similar to Relief Bonds which RBI was issuing previously, on behalf of the Government of India. RBI Relief Bonds are discontinued till further notice. The application for both categories of bonds may be submitted to SBI or HDFC Bank. They issue bond certificates of GOI.

### Distinction between Shares and Debentures

The difference between shares and debentures is given below:

| Shares | Debentures |
|---|---|
| 1. Shareholders are the owners of the company. | Debenture holders are the creditors of the company. |
| 2. Shareholders have voting **rights**, and consequently control the affairs of the company. | Debenture holders have no voting rights and consequently do not pose any threat to the existing control of the company. |
| 3. Shareholders get dividend from the company which depends upon the profits. | Debenture holders get fixed rate of interest irrespective of the profits of the company. |
| 4. Equity shareholders cannot get back their money before liquidation of the company. However, they can sell their shares in the stock market. | Debenture holders get back their money at maturity. They can also sell their debentures in the stock market, if these debentures are listed. |
| 5. Shares cannot be converted into debentures. | Debentures can be converted into equity shares. |
| 6. At the time of liquidation, shareholders are paid at last. | Debenture holders are paid as per preferential order at the time of liquidation. |

## 1.7 CORPORATE VALUATION

The term 'Business' is more comprehensive than the assets employed by it. The valuation of business is to reckon all types of assets as well as liabilities. In recent years, a number of new approaches to measure the value of corporates have been developed and practised. The following table can give the idea of corporate value:

**Table 1.1: World Billionaires (2011)**

| Sr. No. | Name | Country | Business | Value ($ Billion) |
|---|---|---|---|---|
| 1 | Carlos Slim Helu | Mexico | Telecom | 74 |
| 2 | Bill Gates | U.S. | Microsoft | 56 |
| 3 | Warren Buffet | U.S. | Investment | 50 |
| 4 | Bernard Arnault | France | LVMH | 41 |
| 5 | Larry Ellison | U.S. | Oracle | 39.5 |
| 6 | Lakshmi Mittal | India | Steel | 31.1 |
| 7 | Amancio Ortega | Spain | Zara | 31 |
| 8 | Eike Batista | Brazil | Mining | 30 |
| 9 | Mukesh Ambani | India | Oil Petrochem | 27 |
| 10 | Christy Walton | U.S. | Wal-Mart | 26.5 |

***Source:*** Forbes Asia, March 2011.

The above table indicates the top 10 billionaires in the world. The study was conducted by Forbes Asia Magazine, and it was published in the magazine in the month of March 2011. The data relates to the year 2010. The data relates to the corporations with their valuation. The valuation is of the companies and not the individuals. It shows the value created by the companies. It is also the market value of the shares of the companies. The individuals are the leaders or heads of the companies. The value is expressed in U.S. Dollar Billions. The highest valuation is of Carlos Slim Helu of Mexico. There are four Billionaires from U.S. and two from India in the list of top 10. There is a large gap in the value of first and second as compared to others. The highest value creator is involved in telecom business and the 10th one is Wal-Mart involved in, i.e., retail business. The Indian companies have also started figuring in the Billionaires due to globalisation. Thus, Indian companies have also started becoming global companies.

## 1.8 EXERCISES

1. What is Business Valuation? What is its need?
2. Explain the following concepts with the help of examples:
   (a) Book Value (b) Intrinsic Value
   (c) Market Value (d) Economic Value
   (e) Fair Value
3. Why is business valuation exercise undertaken by corporate managers?
4. Explain the purpose of valuation of business.
5. What are equity shares? Why are equity shares issued by the corporates?
6. Explain the difference between shares and debentures.
7. Write short notes:
   (a) Corporate Valuation (b) Shareholder Value Creation
   (c) Market Value of Shares (d) A Public Limited Company

❖ ❖ ❖

# Chapter 2 APPROACHES TO VALUATION

2.1 Introduction
2.2 Assets-based Approach
2.3 Earnings-based Approach
2.4 Market Valuation Approach
2.5 Net Income Approach
2.6 Net Operating Income Approach
2.7 Modigliani and Miller Approach
2.8 Exercises

## 2.1 INTRODUCTION

It is important for the managers to understand the process and methods of valuing the business firm. The term business is more comprehensive than the assets deployed in it. A business valuation is a complex process and it involves a multitude of factors ranging from financial matters to historical perspectives. It is a broad and technically challenging discipline. The valuation is performed in a variety of contexts and for a variety of purposes. The business valuation exercise is akin to the valuation of an asset, a security and is dependent on basic financial concepts of the time value of money, risk and returns and future cash flows. A business valuation will use a variety of business valuation methods to determine a fair price for business. The firms that face an important investment, acquisition or growth decisions, particularly in a rapidly changing competitive environment, effective management requires an understanding of value creation and a command over valuation analysis. While valuing a business, one should not rely on any one method rather than selecting combination of methods that can help to take better decision. Financial experts believe that business valuation using any method should not be too high or too low because that could be costly, resulting in either over payment or lost opportunities. It is the need of the hour that the executives belonging to finance or non-finance background must possess thorough understanding of all the available valuation techniques, because they plan an important role in the various strategic decisions taken by the corporates. The following are the various approaches of valuation of business.

## 2.2 ASSET-BASED APPROACH

Every running business has assets and liabilities a natural way to determine the value of these assets and liabilities. The difference between the value of assets and liabilities is the value of business. This approach focuses on determining the value of net assets from the perspective of equity share valuation. The valuation of assets is based on the going concern concept. The most common asset valuation approaches are as follows:

(i) **Book value approach:** The book value is simply the business valuation based upon the accounting books of the business. Assets less liabilities equals the owner's equity. It is the book value of the assets. However, the problem with book value approach is that the accounting records may not accurately reflect the true value of the assets in the business valuation.

(ii) **Adjusted book value approach:** There are two types of adjusted book value – Tangible Book Value and Economic Book Value. Tangible book value is based on comprising the value of tangible assets only. Assets such as goodwill, patents, capitalised preliminary expenses and deferred revenue expenses are not considered. Economic book value is the value of the business that allows a book value analysis that adjusts the assets to their market value. This includes value of goodwill, real estate inventories and other assets at their market value.

(iii) **Replacement value approach:** This is closely similar to an adjusted book value analysis. Liabilities are deducted from the replacement value of the assets to determine the replacement value of the business. Replacement value of an asset is usually higher than its book value.

(iv) **Liquidation value approach:** This is also similar to an adjusted book value analysis liabilities are deducted from the liquidation value of the assets to determine the liquidation value of the business. A liquidation asset-based approach determines the net cash that would be received if all assets are sold and liabilities paid off.

In order to arrive at the net assets value, total external liabilities are deducted from total assets:

$$\therefore \text{Net Assets} = \text{Total Assets} - \text{Total External Liabilities.}$$

The value of net assets is also known as net assets or shareholder's funds. Assuming the figure of net assets to be positive it implies the value available to equity shareholders after the payment of all external liabilities. The net assets per share can be obtained dividing net assets by the number of equity shares issued and outstanding.

$$\therefore \text{Value per Share} = \frac{\text{Net Assets}}{\text{No. of Equity Shares Issued}}$$

The net assets value is contingent upon the measure of value adopted for the purpose of valuation of assets and liabilities.

**Illustration 2.1:** Following is the balance sheet of 'H' Ltd. as on 31st March, 2012:

| Liabilities | ₹/lakhs | Assets | | ₹/lakhs |
|---|---|---|---|---|
| 40,000, 12% Preference shares of ₹100 each fully paid up | 40 | Fixed Assets | | 120 |
| | | **Current Assets:** | | |
| 12,00,000 Equity shares of 10 each fully paid up | 120 | Stock | 100 | |
| | | Debtors | 50 | |
| Reserve & Surplus | 23 | Cash Bank | 16 | 166 |
| 10% Debentures | 27 | Preliminary Expenses | | 4 |
| Creditors | 70 | | | |
| Provision for tax | 10 | | | |
| | **290** | | | **290** |

A firm of professional values has provided the following market estimates of its various assets:

| Fixed Assets | ₹130 lakhs |
|---|---|
| Stock | 97 lakhs |
| Debtors | 45 lakhs |

All other assets are to be taken at their balance sheet value. The company has not yet declared and paid any dividend on preference shares. The value also estimate the current sale proceeds of the firm's assets, in the event of its liquidation. Fixed assets ₹ 100 lakhs, Stock ₹ 90 lakhs and Debtors ₹ 40 lakhs. Besides the firm is to incur ₹ 0.5 lakhs as liquidation expenses.

You are required to compute the net asset value per share as per book value, market value and liquidation value approaches.

**Solution:** Determination of Net Assets Value per Share

**(a) Book value approach**

| | | ₹/lakhs |
|---|---|---|
| Fixed assets | | 120 |
| Current assets | | 166 |
| Total assets | | 286 |
| *Less*: **External liabilities** | | |
| 10% Debentures | 27 | |
| Creditors | 70 | |
| Prov. for tax | 10 | 107 |
| | | 179 |
| Net assets | | |
| *Less*: Preference capital | 40 | |
| Preference dividend | 4.8 | 44.8 |
| Balance available to equity holders | | 134.2 |

$$\text{Book Value per Share} = \frac{\text{Net Assets}}{\text{No.of Eq.Shares}} = \frac{134.2}{12} = ₹\ 11.20$$

**(b) Market value approach**

| | | |
|---|---|---|
| Fixed assets | | 130 |
| **Current assets:** | | |
| Stock | 97 | |
| Debtors | 45 | |
| Cash bank | 16 | 158 |
| Total assets | | 288 |
| *Less*: **External liabilities** | | |
| Debentures | 27 | |
| Creditors | 70 | |
| Prov. for tax | 10 | 107 |
| Net Assets | | 181 |
| *Less*: Preference capital | | 40 |
| Preference dividend | | 4.8 |
| Balance to equity holders | | 136.2 |

$$\text{Value per Share} = \frac{136.2}{12} = ₹\ 11.35$$

**(c) Liquidation value approach**

| | | |
|---|---|---|
| Fixed assets | | 100 |
| **Current assets:** | | |
| Stock | 90 | |
| Debtors | 40 | |
| Cash bank | 16 | 146 |
| Total Assets | | 246 |
| *Less*: **External liabilities** | | |
| Debentures | 27 | |
| Creditor | 70 | |
| Tax | 10 | |
| Expenses | 0.50 | 107.5 |
| Net assets | | 138.50 |
| *Less*: Preference capital | 40 | |
| Preference dividend | 4.8 | |
| | | 44.80 |
| Balance to Equity holders | | 93.70 |

$$\text{Value per Share} = \frac{93.70}{12} = ₹\ 7.81$$

**Note:** Preliminary expenses are not be considered because it has no realisable or liquidation value.

## 2.3 EARNINGS BASED APPROACH

The earnings approach is essentially guided by the economic position that business valuation should be related to the firm's potential of future carvings. The normal purpose of the contemplated purchase of business is to provide for the buyer the annuity for his investment outlay, the buyer would certainly expect yearly income, returns stable or fluctuating but neverthless.

Some return which commensurate with the price paid therefor. Valuation based on earnings based on the rate of return on capital employed, is a more modern method being adopted. This approach overcomes the limitation of assets-based approach, which ignores the firm's prospects of future earnings and ability to generate cash in business valuation earnings can be expressed in the sense of accounting as well as financial management.

## Income Capitalization

Capital of earning approach determines the business value using a single measure of the expected business economic benefits as the numerator. This is divided by the capitalization rate that represents the risk associated with receiving this benefit in the future. The earnings figure to be capitalized should be one that reflects the true nature of the business such as the last three years average current year or projected year. While determining a capitalization rate there is a need to compare with the rates available to similarly risky investments.

## Dividend Capitalization

While using dividend capitalization method it is necessary to determine dividend paying capacity of business. Dividend paying capacity is based on average net income and average cash flow. In order to determine dividend paying capacity, near term capital needs, expansion plans, debt repayment operation cushion, contractual requirements, past dividend paying history of a business and dividends of a comparable company should also be considered. Thereafter, percentage of average net income and of average cash flow that can be used for payment of dividends can be estimated. On the other hand, capitalization rate includes the risk force rate of return as its core and it is increased by the risk inherent in the business. A company's capitalization rate is often derived by subtracting company's expected long-term annual growth rate from its discount rate. Thus a growing company's capitalization rate is usually lower than its discount rate.

**Illustration 2.2:** A firm has reported a profit of ₹ 67 lakhs after paying taxes @33 per cent, in the current year, on close examination the analyst ascertains that the current year's income includes the following:

(i) An Extraordinary income of ₹ 7 lakhs.

(ii) An Extraordinary loss of ₹ 3 lakhs.

Apart from existing operations, which are normal in nature and are likely to continue in future, the company expects to launch a new product in the coming year. The revenue and cost estimates in respect of the new product are as follows:

| Particulars | ₹ lakhs |
|---|---|
| Sales | 58 |
| Materials cost | 13 |
| Labour cost | 7 |
| Allocated fixed costs | 8 |
| Additional fixed costs | – |

From the given information, compute the value of the business, given that capitalization rate applicable to such business in the market is 15 per cent.

**Solution:**

| Valuation of Business | | | ₹ lakhs |
|---|---|---|---|
| Profit before tax (67 + 33) | | | 100 |
| *Less*: Extraordinary income not likely to accrue in future | | | 7 |
| *Add*: Extraordinary loss (non-recuring) | | | 3 |
| *Add*: **Incremental Income (₹ L)** | | | |
| Sales | | 58 | |
| – Material cost | 13 | | |
| Labour cost | 07 | | |
| Fixed cost | 8 | 28 | 30 |
| Expected profit before tax | | | 126 |
| *Less*: Taxes @33% | | | 42 |
| Future maintainable profits | | | 84 |
| Relevant capitalization factor | | | 15% |

$$\therefore \text{Value of Business} = \frac{84}{15\%} = ₹560 \text{ lakhs}.$$

## 2.4 MARKET VALUATION APPROACH

Market value approach to business valuation attempts to establish the value of business by comparing it to similar business that have recently sold. However, this approach is going to work well only if there are a sufficient number of similar businesses to compare. This approach compares similar companies on a set of variables. Thus, the value of business can be determined by using an industry average such as sales, market price, profit multiple, dividend and times a multiplier. As a result an-industry-specific formula is devised usually based on a multiple of gross sales. The following approaches are used in valuation of business:

**(i) Price-earnings multiple:**

The price-earning ratio is simply the price of a company's share in the stock market divided by its earnings for share. Earning per share is equal to net profit after tax divided by number of equity shares. If there are preference shares, then the preference dividend is deducted from the profit after tax. The value of business is determined as follows:

Value of Business = Market Price per Share × Number of Equity Shares.

Market price per share can be determined with the help of P/E multiple (industry).

**(ii) Dividend capitalization:**

Dividend paying capacity based on average net income and on average cash flow is used. In order to determine dividend paying capacity, near term capital needs, expansion plans, debt repayment, operation cushion, contractual requirements, past dividend paying history of business and dividends of a comparable company can be considered. The value per share can be determined as follows:

$$\text{Value per Share} = \frac{\text{Dividend}}{\text{Capitalisation Rate}}$$

The value of business is determined as follows:

Value per Share × No. of Equity Shares

**(iii) Sales multiple:**

The sales multiple is often used as the business valuation benchmark. The information required is annual sales and an industry multiplier, while is usually a range of .25 to 1 or higher. The industry multiplier can be taken from various financial publications or analyzing sales of similar companies.

**(iv) Profit multiple:**

Profit and sales multiples are the most widely used business valuation benchmarks used in valuing a business. The information needed is pre-tax profits and a market multiplier which may be 1, 2, 3 or 4 and usually a ceiling of 5. The market multiplier can be taken from various financial publications or analyzing the sales of comparative businesses.

**Illustration 2.3:** Determine the value of business on the basis of following data:

| | ₹ |
|---|---|
| Future maintainable profits after taxes | 80,00,000 |
| 1,00,000, 10% Preference shares of ₹ 100 each | 1,00,00,000 |
| 40,00,000 Equity shares of ₹ 10 each | 4,00,00,000 |

P/E Ratio = 8 times.

**Solution:**

(i) Determination of market price of Equity Shares.

| | ₹ |
|---|---|
| Future maintainable profit after tax | 80,00,000 |
| *Less*: Preference Dividend @10% | 10,00,000 |
| Earning to Equity holders | 70,00,000 |
| Number of Equity shares | 40,00,000 |

$$\text{Earnings per Share} = \frac{70{,}00{,}000}{40{,}00{,}000} = ₹\ 1.75$$

P/E Multiple = 8

∴ Market Value per Share = 8 × 1.75

= ₹ 14

(ii) Value of Business = Market Value per Share × No. of Eq. Shares

= ₹ 14 × 40,00,000

= ₹ 56,00,00,000

**Illustration 2.4:** As per financial accounts for the last year, the company has paid dividend @ 20%. The amount of paid up equity capital is ₹ 6,00,000 and 10% preference share capital ₹ 1,00,000. The face value of Equity shares is ₹ 10 and that of the preference shares is ₹ 100. Operating profit is 4,00,000. The tax rate is 30%. The company expects a growth rate of 5% in dividend. Determine the value of firm on the basis:

(a) Dividend Approach

(b) Dividend Growth Approach

assuming that the dividend capitalisation rate is 10%.

**Solution:**

**(a) Dividend approach**

$$\therefore \text{Value of Share} = \frac{D_o}{K}$$

where $D_o$ is the current dividend rate and 'K' is the rate of capitalization.

$$D_1 = 20\% \text{ of } ₹\ 10 = ₹\ 2.$$

$$\therefore \text{Value per Share} = \frac{2}{10\%} = ₹\ 20.$$

$$\text{Value of the Firm} = \text{Value per Share} \times \text{No. of Eq. Shares}$$

$$= 20 \times 60{,}000$$

$$= ₹\ 12{,}00{,}000$$

**(b) Dividend growth approach**

According to dividend growth approach

$$\text{Value per Share} = D_o \frac{(1+g)}{(K-g)}$$

where

$D_o$ = current dividend rate

g = growth rate in dividend

K = capitalization rate.

$$\therefore \text{Value per Share} = \frac{2(1.05)}{(0.10-0.05)} = \frac{2.1}{0.05} = ₹ 42$$

$$\therefore \text{Value of the Firm} = ₹\ 42 \times 60{,}000$$

$$= ₹\ 25{,}20{,}000$$

## 2.5 NET INCOME APPROACH

Net Income Approach of corporate valuation was suggested by Durand. According to him the capital structure decision is relevant to the valuation of the firm. Thus, a change in the financial leverage will lead to the corresponding change in the overall cost of capital as well as the total value of the firm. Therefore, the degree of financial leverage as measured by the ratio of debt-equity ratio is increased, the weighted average cost of capital will decline, while the value of the firm as well as the market price of the equity share will increase. On the other hand, a decrease in the leverage will cause an increase in the overall cost of capital and a decrease both in the value of the firm as well as the market price of the equity shares. The net income approach to valuation is based on the following assumptions:

(i) There are no taxes,

(ii) The cost of debt is less than the equity capitalization rate,

(iii) The use of debt does not change the risk perception of the investors.

**Illustration 2.5:** There are two firms A and B similar in all aspects except in the capital structure employed by them. The financial data for these firms are given below:

| Particulars | Firm 'A' (₹ lakhs) | Firm 'B' (₹ lakhs) |
|---|---|---|
| Net income | 10 | 10 |
| Interest on debt | – | 3 |
| Cost of equity | 10% | 10% |
| Cost of debt | 6% | 6% |

Determine the value of firms and comment on these values:

**Solution:**

| Valuation of firms | (₹ lakhs) | (₹ lakhs) |
|---|---|---|
| **Particulars** | **Firm 'A'** | **Firm 'B'** |
| Net income | 10 | 10 |
| Interest on debt | – | 3 |
| Equity earnings | 10 | 7 |
| ∴ Market value of equity | 100 | 70 |
| ∴ Market value of debit | – | 50 |
| ∴ Value of firm | 100 | 120 |

$$\text{Average cost of capital of Firm 'A'} = \frac{10}{100} \times 100 = 10\%$$

$$\text{Average cost of capital of Firm 'B'} = \frac{10}{120} \times 100 = 8.33\%$$

Firm 'A' is not using debit so it is unleveraged firm and Firm 'B' is using debit and hence, it is a leveraged company. The value of firm having leverage is higher. Hence, in order to increase the value of the firm, it should include debit capital in its capital structure.

**Illustration 2.6:** The net income of X Ltd. for the year is ₹ 50,000. It has ₹ 2,00,000, 10% debt in its capital structure. The equity capitalisation rate is 12.5%. The firm has decided to raise ₹ 1,00,000 by issue of Debentures. The cost of debt and equity will remain unchanged. Determine the value of firm before and after raising the debt.

**Solution:**

**(a) Value of firm before raising debt**

| Particulars | ₹ |
|---|---|
| Net income | 50,000 |
| *Less*: interest | 20,000 |
| Earnings available to equity holders | **30,000** |
| Equity capitalisation rate | 12.5% |
| ∴ Market value of equity (30,000 ÷ 12.5%) | 2,40,000 |
| Market value of debt | 2,00,000 |
| Value of the firm | **4,40,000** |

$$\text{Overall cost of capital} = \frac{50,000}{4,40,000} \times 100 = 11.36\%$$

**(b) Value of firm after raising debt**

| Particular | ₹ |
|---|---|
| Net income | 50,000 |
| – Interest | 30,000 |
| Earnings available to equity holders | **20,000** |
| Equity capitalisation rate | 12.5% |
| ∴ Market value of equity (20,000 ÷ 12.5%) | 1,60,000 |
| Market value of debt | 3,00,000 |
| ∴ Value of firm | **4,60,000** |

$$\text{Overall cost of capital} = \frac{50,000}{4,60,000} \times 100 = 10.9\%$$

The use of additional debt has resulted in increasing the value of the firm and decreasing the overall cost of capital.

## 2.6 NET OPERATING INCOME APPROACH

Net Operating Income approach is another theory of capital structure, suggested by Durand. This approach is opposite to the Net Income approach. The essence of this approach is that the capital structure decision of a firm is irrelevant. The overall capitalisation rate and the cost of debt remain constant for all degrees of leverage. Any change in leverage will not lead to any change in the total value of the firm. The market price of shares as well as the overall cost of capital is independent of the degree of leverage. The value of the firm is determined as follows:

$$V = \frac{EBIT}{K_o}$$

EBIT is the earnings before interest and taxes, i.e., net operating income.

$K_o$ is the overall cost of capital.

**Illustration 2.7:** Yash Ltd. has annual operating income of ₹ 50,000 and the cost of debt is 10% and the outstanding debt is ₹ 2,00,000. The overall capitalisation rate is 12.5%. If the company decides to raise the amount of debt by ₹ 1,00,000 determine the value of the company before and after raising debt. Determine the value of the company and equity capitalisation rate before and after raising the debt.

**Solution:**

**(a) Net Operating Income Approach**

| Value of the firm before raising debt | ₹ |
|---|---|
| Net operating income (EBIT) | 50,000 |
| Overall capitalisation rate | 12.5% |
| ∴ Market value of the firm (4,50,000 ÷ 12.5%) | 4,00,000 |
| ∴ Value of debt | 2,00,000 |
| ∴ Market value of equity | **2,00,000** |

$$\therefore \text{Equity Capitalisation Rate} = \frac{\text{Earning Available}}{\text{M.V. of Equity}} \times 100$$

$$= \frac{50{,}000 - 20{,}000}{2{,}00{,}000} \times 100$$

$$= \frac{30{,}000}{2{,}00{,}000} \times 100 = 15\%.$$

**(b) Valuation of firm when debt is raised**

| | ₹ |
|---|---|
| Net operating income | 50,000 |
| Overall capitalisation rate | 12.5% |
| ∴ Market value of firm (50,000 ÷ 12.5%) | 4,00,000 |
| ∴ Market value of debt | 3,00,000 |
| ∴ Market value of equity | **1,00,000** |

$$\therefore \text{Equity Capitalisation Rate} = \frac{50{,}000 - 30{,}000}{1{,}00{,}000} \times 100$$

$$= \frac{20{,}000}{1{,}00{,}000} \times 100$$

$$= 20\%.$$

The value of the firm remains the same but the equity capiatlisation rate goes up to 20% if additional debt is raised.

**Illustration 2.8:** Two firms A and B are similar in all aspects except the financial leverage employed by them. The relevant financial data for these firms are given below:

| | Firm A (₹ lakhs) | Firm B (₹ lakhs) |
|---|---|---|
| Net operating income | 10 | 10 |
| Overall capitalisation rate | 15% | 15% |
| Debt | 10 | 30 |
| Cost of debt | 10% | 10% |

You are required to determine the value of the firm and equity capitalisation rates using Net Operating Income Approach.

**Solution: Net Operating Income Approach**

| | Firm A (₹ lakhs) | Firm B (₹ lakhs) |
|---|---|---|
| Net operating income | 10 | 10 |
| Overall capitalisation rate | 15% | 15% |
| ∴ Market value of firm (10 ÷ 15%) | 66.67 | 66.67 |
| Value of debt | 10.00 | 30.00 |
| ∴ Market value of equity | **56.67** | **36.67** |

$$\text{Equity Capitalisation Rate} = \frac{\text{Eequity Earnings}}{\text{M.V. of Equity}} \times 100$$

| | | |
|---|---|---|
| Net operating income | 10 | 10 |
| – Interest | 1 | 3 |
| Equity earnings | **9** | **7** |
| ∴ Equity Capitalisation Rate | $= \frac{9}{56.67} \times 100$ =15.9% | $= \frac{7}{66.67} \times 100$ = 19.1% |

The value of firms remains the same but the equity capitalisation rate changes.

## 2.7 MODIGLIANI AND MILLER APPROACH

Franco Modigliani and Merton Miller have developed a new approach of corporate valuation. It is also called as MM approach. They have developed relation between the capital structure, cost of capital and valuation. The MM proposition supports the NOI Approach relating to the independence of the cost of capital of the degree of leverage at any level of debt equity ratio. This approach maintains that the weighted average (overall) cost of capital does not change, with a change in the proportion of debt to equity in the capital structure. The three basic propositions of MM approach are given below:

(a) The overall cost of capital ($K_o$) and the value of firm (V) are independent of its capital structure. The $K_o$ and V are constant for all degrees of leverage. The total value of the firm is given by capitalising the expected stream of operating income at a discount rate appropriate for its risk class.

(b) The cost of equity ($K_e$) is equal to the capitalisation rate of a pure equity stream plus a premium for financial risk equal to the difference between the pure equity capitalisation rate and $K_i$ times the ratio of debt to equity.

(c) The cut-off rate for investment purposes is completely independent of the way in which an investment is financed.

The MM approach is based on the following assumptions:

(i) The capital markets are perfect.

(ii) All investors have the same expectation of firm's net operating income with which to evaluate the value of firm.

(iii) Business risk is equal among all firms within similar operating environment.

(iv) The dividend payout ratio is 100 per cent.

(v) There are no taxes, however, this assumption was removed later on.

**Illustration 2.9:** Two firms X and Y which are identical in all aspects except that firm X has 10% debt of ₹ 5,00,000. The earning before interest and taxes (EBIT) of both the firms are equal, i.e., ₹ 1,20,000. The equity capitalisation rate of X is 16% and that of Y is 15%. Determine the value of firms, using MM Approach.

**Solution: MM Approach Valuation of Firms**

| | ₹ | |
|---|---|---|
| **Particulars** | **X** | **Y** |
| EBIT | 1,20,000 | 1,20,000 |
| – Interest | 50,000 | – |
| Earnings available to equity holder | **70,000** | **1,20,000** |
| Equity capitalisation rate | 16% | 15% |
| Market value of equity | 4,37,500 | 8,00,000 |
| Market value debt | 5,00,000 | – |
| Value of firms | **9,37,500** | **8,00,000** |
| Overall Capitalisation Rate | $= \frac{1,20,000}{9,37,500} \times 100$ | $= \frac{12,00,000}{8,00,000} \times 100$ |
| | = 12.80% | = 15% |

**Illustration 2.10:** Two firms A and B are similar in all respects except in their capital structure. Firm A is an unlevered firm financed by equity only whereas firm B is a levered firm financed by a mix of equity and debt. Relevant particulars of the two firms are given below:

| **Particulars** | **Firm A ₹ lakhs** | **Firm B ₹ lakhs** |
|---|---|---|
| Operating income | 15 | 15 |
| Debt | – | 50 |
| Cost of debt | 12% | 12% |
| Cost of equity | 15% | 16% |

Determine the value of firms using MM Approach.

**Solution:** Value of firm using MM Approach:

| Particular | Firm A ₹ lakhs | Firm B ₹ lakhs |
|---|---|---|
| Operating income | 15 | 15 |
| – Interest | – | 06 |
| Equity earning | **15** | **09** |
| Cost of equity | 0.15 | 0.16 |
| ∴ Market value of equity | 100 | 56.25 |
| Market value of debt | – | 50.00 |
| Value of firm | **100** | **106.25** |
| Overall Capitalisation Rate | $= \frac{15}{100} \times 100$ = 15% | $= \frac{15}{106.25} \times 100$ = 14.42% |

**Illustration 2.11:** A Ltd. has issued 10 lakh Equity shares of ₹ 10 each fully paid up. It has declared dividend during the past five year as follows:

| Year | Rate of Dividend (%) |
|---|---|
| 2006-7 | 12 |
| 2007-8 | 14 |
| 2008-9 | 20 |
| 2009-10 | 21 |
| 2010-11 | 24 |

The average rate of return prevailing in the same industry is 15%. Calculate the value per share and value of A Ltd. based on dividend yield.

**Solution:**

(a) As the dividend has been growing year offer year, it is better to take weighted average of dividends

| Year | Rate of Dividend (%) | Weight | product |
|---|---|---|---|
| 2006.7 | 12 | 1 | 12 |
| 2007.8 | 14 | 2 | 28 |
| 2008.9 | 20 | 3 | 60 |
| 2009.10 | 21 | 4 | 84 |
| 2010.11 | 24 | 5 | 120 |
| | | **15** | **304** |

$$\text{Weighted Average} = \frac{\text{Product}}{\text{Total Weight}}$$

$$= \frac{304}{15} = 20.26\%$$

(b) $\text{Value per Share} = \dfrac{\text{Company's Rate of Dividend}}{\text{Industry Normal}} \times \text{Face Value}$

$$= \frac{20.26}{15} \times 10 = ₹13.50$$

(c) Value of Firm = 10 lakhs × 13.50
= ₹ 135 lakhs

**Illustration 2.12:** Shyam Ltd. and Sundar Ltd. are identical in all respect including risk factors except for debt/equity mix. Shyam Ltd. has issued 12% Debentures of ₹ 300 lakhs, while Sunder Ltd. has issued only equity capital. Both the companies earn 20% before interest and taxes on their total assets of ₹ 500 lakhs. Assuming the corporate tax rate of 30% and capitalization rate of 15% for an all equity company, compute the value companies using (a) Net Income Approach and (b) Net Operating Income Approach

**Solution:**

**(a) Valuation of Companies under Net Income Approach**

| | ₹ lakhs | |
|---|---|---|
| **Particulars** | **Shyam Ltd.** | **Sunder Ltd.** |
| Profit before interest taxes | 100 | 100 |
| – Interest on debentures | 36 | – |
| Profit before tax | 64 | 100 |
| *Less*: Tax 30% | 19.20 | 30 |
| Net income available to equity shareholder | 44.80 | 70 |
| Market value of equity | 299 | 467 |
| Market value of debt | 300 | – |
| Value of firm | **599** | **467** |

**(b) Value of Companies under Net Operating Income Approach**

| | ₹ lakhs | |
|---|---|---|
| **Particulars** | **Shyam Ltd.** | **Sunder Ltd.** |
| Capitalisation of earning @ 15% ($\frac{100}{15} \times 100$) | 667 | 667 |
| *Less*: Value of debt | 210 | – |
| Value of equity | 457 | 667 |
| Value of debt | 300 | – |
| Value of firm | **757** | **667** |

**Note:** EBIT = 20% of 500 lakhs = ₹ 100 lakhs.

**Illustration 2.13:** The following is related to Oriental Ltd.:

| | |
|---|---|
| Net operating Income | ₹ 2,000 lakhs |
| Corporate tax rate | 30% |
| Market value of debt | ₹ 3,000 lakhs |
| Capitalisation rate applicable to a debt free firm in the risk class to which Oriental Ltd. belongs: | 16 per cent. |

What will be the value of Oriental Ltd. according to the MM approach?

**Solution:** According to MM Approach value of the firm is:

$$V = O\frac{(1-t)}{r} + tD$$

where

V = Value of firm

r = Capitalisation rate

t = Tax rate

D = Amount of debt

$$\therefore V = \frac{O(1-t)}{r} + tD$$

$$= \frac{2000\ (1-0.3)}{0.16} + (0.3 \times 30{,}00)$$

$$= \frac{1{,}400}{0.16} + 900$$

$$= 8{,}750 + 900$$

$$= ₹\ 9{,}650 \text{ lakhs.}$$

**Illustration 2.14:** The following information is available for A Ltd.

| | |
|---|---|
| Net operating income | ₹ 400 lakhs |
| Interest on debt | ₹ 100 lakhs |
| Cost of equity | 18% |
| Cost of debt | 12% |

(a) Determine the value of A Ltd. and overall cost of capital.

(b) A Ltd. employs an additional debt of ₹ 1,000 lakhs to finance a project which earns an operating income of ₹ 200 lakhs. There are no taxes and net operating income approach is to be applied. Determine the revised value of A Ltd. and revised overall cost of capital.

**Solution:**

**(a) Value of Firm**

| | **₹ lakhs** |
|---|---|
| Net operating income | 400 |
| – Interest on debt | 100 |
| Equity earnings | 300 |
| ∴ Market value of equity $(\frac{300}{18\%})$ | 1,667 |
| ∴ Market value of debt | 833 |
| Value of firm | **2,500** |

$$\text{Over all Cost of Capital} = \frac{400}{2{,}500} \times 100 = 16\%$$

**(b) Revised Value of Firm**

| | ₹ lakhs |
|---|---|
| Net operating income | 600 |
| – Interest on debt | 220 |
| Equity earnings | 380 |
| ∴ Market value of equity $(\frac{300}{18} \times 100)$ | 2,111 |
| Market value of debt | 1,833 |
| Value of firm | **3,944** |

$$\text{Over all Cost of Capital} = \frac{600}{3,944} \times 100 = 15.21\%$$

**Illustration 2.15:** The following information is available for A Ltd.

| | ₹ lakhs |
|---|---|
| Net operating income | 400 |
| Interest on debt | 100 |
| Cost of equity | 15% |
| Cost of debt | 12% |

(a) What is the value of A Ltd. using NOI Approach?

(b) Find the value of A Ltd. if it employs ₹ 100 lakhs of debt to finance a project which earns an operating income of ₹ 200 lakhs. Assume that there are no taxes.

**Solutions:**

**(a) Value of A Ltd. (NOI Approach)**

| | ₹ lakhs |
|---|---|
| Net operating income | 400 |
| – Interest on debt | 100 |
| Equity earnings | 300 |
| ∴ Market value of equity $(\frac{300}{15\%})$ | 2,000 |
| Market value of debt $(\frac{100}{12\%})$ | 833 |
| Value of firm | **2,833** |

**(b) Revised Valuation**

| | ₹ lakhs |
|---|---|
| Net operating income (400 + 200) | 600 |
| – Interest on debt | 112 |
| Equity earning | 488 |
| ∴ Market value of equity $(\frac{488}{15\%})$ | 3,247 |
| Market value of debt | 933 |
| Total value of firm | **4,180** |

**Illustration 2.16:** Raj Ltd. and Taj Ltd. belong to the same risk class. These companies are identical in all respects except that Raj Ltd. has no debt in the capital structure but Taj Ltd. employs debt in its capital structure. The relevant financial data of the two companies are given below:

| | ₹ lakhs | |
|---|---|---|
| | **Raj Ltd.** | **Taj Ltd.** |
| Net operating income | 10 | 10 |
| Interest and debt | – | 3 |
| Equity capitalisation rate | 14% | 18% |
| Debt capitalisation rate | – | 10% |

Pankaj owns ₹ 1 lakh worth of Raj's equity. What arbitrage will he resort to?

**Solution: Valuation of Firms**

| | ₹ lakhs | |
|---|---|---|
| | **Raj Ltd.** | **Taj Ltd.** |
| Net operating income | 10 | 10 |
| *Less*: Interest | – | 3 |
| Equity earnings | 10 | 7 |
| Market value of equity | 71.42 | 38.88 |
| Market value of debt | – | 30.00 |
| Market value of firm | **71.42** | **68.88** |
| Average cost of capital (NOI ÷ Total capital) × 100 | 14% | 14.52% |

As a rational investor Pankaj should sell his equity in Raj Ltd. and invest in Taj Ltd. because its equity capitalisation as well as overall capitalisation rate is higher.

**Illustration 2.17:** The EBIT of Sweet Ltd. is ₹ 2,00,000. The income tax rate is 35%. Other data is as follows:

| Debt ₹ | Cost of Debt before tax % | Cost of Equity |
|---|---|---|
| 1,00,000 | 10.0 | 12.0 |
| 2,00,000 | 10.5 | 12.0 |
| 3,00,000 | 11.0 | 12.6 |
| 4,00,000 | 12.0 | 13.0 |
| 5,00,000 | 14.0 | 13..6 |

Determine the amount of debt that should be used by the company in its capital structure in order to maximize its value.

**Solution: Valuation of Firm**

| EBIT | Int | NI | Taxes | EAT | $K_d$ | $K_e$ | O | S | Value |
|---|---|---|---|---|---|---|---|---|---|
| 2,00,000 | 10,000 | 1,90,000 | 66,500 | 1,23,500 | 6.5 | 12 | 1,00,000 | 10,29,167 | 11,29,167 |
| 2,00,000 | 21,000 | 1,79,000 | 62,500 | 1,16,350 | 6.8 | 12.6 | 2,00,000 | 9,23,413 | 11,25,413 |
| 2,00,000 | 33,000 | 1,67,000 | 58,450 | 1,08,550 | 7.1 | 13 | 3,00,000 | 8,35,000 | 11,35,000 |
| 2,00,000 | 48,000 | 1,52,000 | 53,200 | 98,800 | 7.8 | 13.6 | 4,00,000 | 7,26,471 | 11,26,471 |
| 2,00,000 | 70,000 | 1,30,000 | 45,500 | 84,300 | 9.1 | 15.6 | 5,00,000 | 5,41,667 | 10,41,667 |

The maximum value of firm is ₹ 11,35,000 when the amount of debt is ₹ 3,00,000. Thus, the firm should used ₹ 3,00,000 as a debt to maximize the value of the firm.

**Note:** $K_d$ = Cost of Debt (Int Tax) = (I – t)

= (10 – 35%)

= 10 – 3.5 = 6.5%.

**Illustration 2.18:** The current operating income of Zed Ltd. is ₹ 4,00,000. The company has ₹ 10,00,000 of 10% debt outstanding. Its cost of equity capital is estimated to be 15 p.c. The company is considering increasing its leverage by raising an additional ₹ 5,00,000 debt and using the proceeds to retire that amount of equity. As a result of increased financial risk, the cost of debt is likely to go up to 12% and cost of equity to 18 per cent. Would you advise the company to recommend the plan?

**Solution:**

**(a) Valuation of Firm at Present**

| | |
|---|---|
| EBIT | ₹ 4,00,000 |
| – Interest | 1,00,000 |
| Earning to equity holders | 3,00,000 |
| Equity capitalisation rate | 15% |
| ∴ Market value of equity | 20,00,000 |
| Market value of debt | 10,00,000 |
| Value of firm | **30,00,000** |

$$\text{Overall Cost of Capital} = \frac{4,00,000}{30,00,000} \times 100 = 13.33\%$$

**(b) Valuation of (Proposed) Firm**

| | |
|---|---|
| EBIT | ₹ 4,00,000 |
| – Interest | 1,80,000 |
| Earning to equity holders | 2,20,000 |
| Equity capitalisation rate | 18% |
| ∴ Market value of equity | 12,20,000 |
| Market Value of debt | 15,00,000 |
| Total Value of firm | **27,22,000** |

$$\text{Over all Cost of Capital} = \frac{4,00,000}{27,22,000} \times 100 = 13\%$$

The proposal cannot be recommended because the total value of the firm is reduced from ₹ 30 lakhs to ₹ 27.22 lakhs.

**Illustration 2.19:** The following information is available for two companies K Ltd. and P Ltd. for the year ended on 31st March, 2012.

| | **'K' Ltd. (₹)** | **'P' Ltd. (₹)** |
|---|---|---|
| Net operating income | 2,00,000 | 3,00,000 |
| Interest | – | 50,000 |
| Cost of debt | 10% | 10% |
| Cost of equity | 15% | 15% |

Calculate:

(a) Market value of cash firm
(b) Market value of equity of each firm
(c) Average cost of capital
(d) Market value of 'K' Ltd. if it employs ₹ 30 lakhs debt to finance a project that yields an operating income of ₹ 4 lakhs
(e) Market value of 'P' Ltd. if it sells ₹ 3 lakhs of additional equity and retires ₹ 3 lakhs of outstanding debt.

**Solution:**

**(a) Valuation of Firms**

| | ₹ lakhs | |
|---|---|---|
| | **'K' Ltd.** | **'P' Ltd.** |
| Net operating income | 2 | 3 |
| – Interest | – | 0.50 |
| Equity earnings | **2** | **2.50** |

| | | 'K' Ltd. | 'P' Ltd. |
|---|---|---|---|
| **(b)** | Market Value of Equity | 13.33 | 76.67 |
| | Market value of debt | – | 5.00 |
| | (a) Market value of firm | 13.33 | 21.67 |
| **(c)** | Average Cost of Capital | | |
| | $= \frac{\text{Net Operating Income}}{\text{M.V. of Capital}}$ | $= \frac{2}{13.33} \times 100$ | $= \frac{3}{21.67} \times 100$ |
| | | = 15% | = 13.85% |

**(d) Valuation of 'K' Ltd.**

| | **₹ lakhs** |
|---|---|
| Net operating income | 6 |
| – Interest | 3 |
| Equity earnings | 3 |
| Cost of equity | 15% |
| ∴ Market value of equity | 20 |
| Market value of debt | 30 |
| Market value of firm | **50** |

**(e) Valuation of 'P' Ltd.**

| | **₹ lakhs** |
|---|---|
| Net operating income | 3.00 |
| – Interest | 0.20 |
| Equity earning | 2.80 |
| Equity capitalisation rate | 15% |
| Market value of equity | 187 |
| Market value of debt | 2 |
| Market value of firm | **189** |

**Illustration 2.20:** The following is the Balance sheet of Yash Ltd. as on 31st March, 2012.

| Liabilities | ₹ lakhs | Assets | ₹ lakhs |
|---|---|---|---|
| Equity Share Capital | | Land and Buildings | 50 |
| (₹ 10 each fully paid) | 100 | Plant and Machinery | 90 |
| Reserve & Surplus | 50 | Marketable Securities | 10 |
| Current Liabilities | 50 | Stock | 20 |
| | | Debtors | 25 |
| | | Cash Bank | 05 |
| | **200** | | **200** |

Net profit before tax amounted to ₹ 74 lakhs including ₹ 4 lakhs as extraordinary income. Besides, the company has earned interest income of ₹ 2 lakhs from investments in marketable securities. It is not usual for the firm to have excess cash and invest in marketable securities. However, an additional amount of ₹ 10 lakh per annum will be required to be spent on advertisement for the smooth running of the business in the year to come.

Market value of Land and Buildings and Plant and Machinery are estimated at ₹ 100 lakh and ₹ 110 lakhs respectively. In order to match the revalued figures of these fixed assets, additional depreciation of ₹ 10 lakhs is required to be taken into consideration, effective corporate tax may be taken at 30 per cent. The capitalization rate applicable to business of such risks is 15 per cent. Determine the value of the firm.

**Solution: Value of Business**

| | | ₹ lakhs |
|---|---|---|
| Profit before tax | | 74 |
| *Less*: (i) Extraordinary income | 4 | |
| (ii) Addition on depreciation | 10 | |
| (iii) Advertisement cost | 10 | |
| (iv) Interest on securities | 2 | 26 |
| EBIT | | 48 |
| *Less*: Taxes @ 30% | | 14.40 |
| Future maintainable profits | | 33.60 |
| Capitalisation rate | | 15% |
| ∴ Value of business | | **224.00** |

**Illustration 2.21:** The value of two firms X and Y in accordance with the traditional theory are given below:

| **Particulars** | **X (₹)** | **Y (₹)** |
|---|---|---|
| Operating income | 5,00,000 | 5,00,000 |
| – Interest | – | 1,00,000 |
| Net income | 5,00,000 | 4,00,000 |
| Cost of equity | 10% | 11% |
| Market value of equity | 50,00,000 | 36,00,000 |
| Market value of debt | – | 20,00,000 |
| Market value of firm | 50,00,000 | 56,00,000 |
| ∴ Average cost of capital | 10% | 9% |
| Debt equity ratio | 0 | 0.556 |

Compute the value of firms X and Y as per MM approach. Assume that corporate income tax does not exist and the equilibrium values of $K_o$ (cost capitalization) is 12.5%.

**Solution: Valuation of Firm**

| Particulars | X (₹) | Y (₹) |
|---|---|---|
| Operating income | 5,00,000 | 50,00,000 |
| – Interest | – | 1,00,000 |
| Net income for equity holders | 5,00,000 | 4,00,000 |
| Equilibrium cost of capital | 12.5% | 12.5% |
| ∴ Value of firm | 40,00,000 | 40,00,000 |
| – Market value debt | – | 20,00,000 |
| Market value of equity | 40,00,000 | 20,00,000 |
| ∴ Cost of Equity | $= \frac{5,00,000}{40,00,000} \times 100$ | $= \frac{4,00,000}{20,00,000} \times 100$ |
| | = 12.5% | = 20% |

## 2.8 EXERCISES

1. What do you mean by Valuation Approach?
2. How would you determine the following?
   (a) The cost of equity in the NOI Approach.
   (b) Value of equity given the equity capitalisation rate, EBIT and Interest.
   (c) The overall capitalisation rate.
   (d) Value of levered firm under MM Approach.
   (e) Cost of Debt.
3. What is MM Approach? Is the MM approach realistic with respect to capital structure and the value of the firm?
4. What is Market Value Approach of valuation of a firm?
5. What is Net Income Approach of Valuation of Business?
6. How is Net Operating Income Approach different from Net Income Approach?
7. Write short notes on:
   (a) Cost of Equity (b) Overall Capitalisation Rate
   (c) Earnings Approach (d) Net Assets Value Approach.
8. Explain the difference between market value of equity and value of equity shares of company.
9. X Ltd. and Y Ltd. are identical in every respect except that X Ltd. is unlevered while Y Ltd. is levered company. Y Ltd. has ₹ 20 lakh of 8% Debentures outstanding. The EBIT of both the companies is ₹ 6 lakh and tax rate is 35 per cent. If the equity capitalisation rate is 10 per cent, determine the value of companies, using MM Approach.
   (Answer: $V_x$ = ₹ 39 lakh, $V_y$ = ₹ 46 lakh)

10. The Balance Sheet of Bee Ltd. as on 31st March, 2012 is as follows:

| Liabilities | | Assets | |
|---|---|---|---|
| Equity Share Capital (₹ 10 each) | 200 | Plant and Machinery | 250 |
| | | Land and Building | 150 |
| Reserve and Surplus | 180 | Stock | 80 |
| 12% Debentures | 150 | Debtors | 60 |
| Creditors | 35 | Cash Bank | 40 |
| Other Current Liabilities | 15 | | |
| | **580** | | **580** |

The market value of assets as assessed by the professional value is as follows:

| | |
|---|---|
| Plant and Machinery | ₹ 180 lakhs |
| Land and Building | ₹ 300 lakhs |

Other assets are valued at Book Value. You are required to compute the (a) value of firm and (b) value of equity share of the company.

(Answer: V = ₹ 610 lakhs, value per equity share ₹ 23)

11. Akansha Ltd. has an issued and paid up and equity capital of 5,00,000 shares of ₹ 10 each. The company declared a dividend of ₹ 12.50 lakhs during the last 5 year and expects to maintain the same level of dividends in future also. The average dividend yield for listed companies in the same line of business is 18%. Calculate the value of business.

(Answer: V = ₹ 69.45)

12. Two firms A and B are similar in all aspects except in the capital structure employed by them. Financial data of these firms are given below:

| | Firm A (₹) | Firm B (₹) |
|---|---|---|
| Operating income | 10,000 | 10,000 |
| Interest on debt | 0 | 3,000 |
| Cost of equity | 10% | 10% |
| Cost of debt | 6% | 6% |

Determine the value of firms using Net Income Approach.

(Answer: VA ₹ 1,00,000, VB ₹ 1,20,000)

13. Two firms X and Y are similar in all aspects except the financial leverage employed by them. Relevant data for these firms are given below:

| | Firm X (₹) | Firm Y (₹) |
|---|---|---|
| Net operating income | 1,00,000 | 1,00,000 |
| Interest on debt | 10,000 | 30,000 |
| Overall capitalisation rate | 15% | 15% |
| Debt capitalisation rate | 10% | 10% |

Determine the value of firms, using Net Operating Income Approach.

(Answer: $V_x$ = ₹ 6.67 lakh, $V_y$ = ₹ 6.67 lakh)

14. The financial data of two firms are given below:

| Particulars | Firm 'A' (₹ lakhs) | Firm 'B' (₹ lakhs) |
|---|---|---|
| EBIT | 1.50 | 1.50 |
| Interest | – | 0.60 |
| Cost of Equity | 15% | 16% |
| Cost of Debt | – | 12% |

Mr. Prakash owns 10% Equity in firm 'B'. What arbitrage will he resort to?

(Answer: The value of levered firm B is higher than that of unlevered firm 'A'. In such a situation, MM cannot persist because equity investor would do well to sell their equity in firm B and invest in firm 'A'. Mr. Prakash should sell his equity in 'B' and invest in the equity as well as debt of firm A)

15. The following information is available for two firms 'B' and 'C' Ltd.

| Particulars | B Ltd. (₹ lakhs) | C Ltd. (₹ lakhs) |
|---|---|---|
| Net Operating Income | 20 | 30 |
| Interest on Debt | – | 10 |
| Cost of Equity | 15% | 15% |
| Cost of Debt | 10% | 10% |

Determine the market value of Equity Market Value of Debt and Market Value of Firms.

(a) What is the average cost of capital of cash firm?

(b) What happens to the average cost of capital of B Ltd. if it employs ₹ 300 lakh of debt to finance a project that yields an operating income of ₹ 40 lakhs?

(c) What happens to the average cost of capital of 'C' Ltd. if it sells ₹ 100 lakh of additional equity at par to retire 100 lakh of outstanding debt?

(Answer: Me – B ₹ 133 lakh, C – ₹ 133 lakh, Md = B – ₹ Nil, C – ₹ 100 lakh, (a) B – 15%, C – 13% (b) B – 12% (c) C – 20%)

# Chapter 3 DISCOUNTED CASH FLOW VALUATION

3.1 Introduction
3.2 Discounted Cash Flow
3.3 Discounted Cash Flow Valuation
3.4 Operating Free Cash Flows
3.5 Exercises

## 3.1 INTRODUCTION

Traditionally, the adjusted book value approach was used more commonly for valuation for business. However, there were certain difficulties. The accuracy of the book values depends on how well the net book values of the assets reflect their fair market values. Inflation drives a wedge between the book value of an asset and its current value. Some assets become obsolete and worthless even before they are fully depreciated in the books. The net assets valuation based on book value is in tune with the going concern principle of accounting. Liquidation value measure is guided by the realisable value available on the winding up of a company. Again, the price-earning ratio approach as a measure of valuation of equity shareholder's wealth is essentially based on accounting profits or earnings. The earnings approach is essentially guided by the economic proposition that business valuation should be related to the firm's potential of future earnings. Accordingly, there are two major variants of earnings measure on accounting basis and earnings measure on cash flow basis.

Discounted cash flow approach is used to evaluate capital expenditure proposals in terms of their potential for creating net present value for the firm. The objective of the firm is to create wealth by using existing and future resources to produce goods and services. In order to create wealth, the discounted cash flows must exceed the present value of cash outflows. This method considers the time value of money concept and hence, it is considered better for evaluation of business proposals. In case of mutually exclusive in investments, this method is more useful.

## 3.2 DISCOUNTED CASH FLOW

Cash flows means cash inflows in the business as well as cash outflows from the business over a period of time. Every business involves cash outflow initially, i.e., investment in fixed assets as well as current assets. This investment generates cash in future through sales or other incomes. These cash flows are received over a period of time in future. These future cash flows should be discounted at certain discount rate in order to arrive at present value. Comparing cash outflows with future cash flows is not an ideal solution because of time period. The money receivable at the end of one year, its present value is definitely less. Hence, future cash flows are discounted, normally at cost of capital. Thus, the net present value is obtained by discounting all cash inflows and outflows attributable to capital investment. For this purpose, the rate of discount is chosen suitably. This method involves the followings stages:

(i) Calculation of cash flows,
(ii) Discounting cash flows by a discount factor,
(iii) Aggregating the discount cash inflows and comparing them with the total discounted cash outflows.

**Illustration 3.1:** X Ltd. is currently under evaluation of a project which will yield the following returns over a period of time:

| Year | Gross Income (₹) |
|---|---|
| 1 | 80,000 |
| 2 | 80,000 |
| 3 | 90,000 |
| 4 | 90,000 |
| 5 | 75,000 |

Cost of machine to be installed amounts to ₹ 2,00,000. The machine is to be depreciated at 20% per annum at written down value method. The income tax rate is 30%. If the cost of capital is 10%. Would you recommend accepting the project using discounted cash flow method?

**Solution:**

(a) Calculation of Cash Flow after Tax (₹)

| Year | Gross Income | Depreciation | Balance | Income Tax @30% | Net Cash Flow | CFAT |
|---|---|---|---|---|---|---|
| 1 | 80,000 | 40,000 | 40,000 | 12,000 | 28,000 | 68,000 |
| 2 | 80,000 | 32,000 | 48,000 | 14,400 | 33,600 | 65,600 |
| 3 | 90,000 | 25,600 | 64,400 | 19,320 | 45,080 | 70,680 |
| 4 | 90,000 | 20,480 | 69,520 | 20,856 | 48,664 | 69,144 |
| 5 | 75,000 | 16,384 | 58,616 | 17,585 | 41,031 | 57,415 |

**Note:** Depreciation is added back to determine cash flows.

(b) Calculation of Net Present Value

| Year | CFAT | D.F. @10% | Present Value (₹) |
|---|---|---|---|
| 1 | 68,000 | 0.09091 | 61,818 |
| 2 | 65,600 | 0.8264 | 54,212 |
| 3 | 70,680 | 0.7513 | 53,102 |
| 4 | 69,144 | 0.6830 | 48,274 |
| 5 | 57,415 | 0.6210 | 35,655 |
| Present value of cash inflows | | | 3,56,547 |
| Present value of cash outflows | | | 2,00,000 |
| ∴ Net present value | | | **1,56,574** |

The Net present value is positive and very high, therefore, project is strongly recommended.

## 3.3 DISCOUNTED CASH FLOW VALUATION APPROACH

Valuation of firm using discounted cash flow is a more scientific and systematic way of valuation of business. However, a firm is viewed as a growing entity and for valuing it, it is necessary to take into account all the investments in fixed assets and net working capital that are expected to be made over time to sustain growth of the firm, Thus, valuing a firm using the discounted cash flow approach calls for forecasting cash flows over an indefinite period of time for an entity that is expected to grow. The discounted cash flow approach to valuing firm involves the following steps:

(a) Forecast the cash flow during the explicit forecast period,
(b) Establish the cost of capital,
(c) Determine the continuing value at the end of the explicit forecast period,
(d) Calculate the value of firm.

The value of a firm is determined as follows:

$$V = \sum_{t=1}^{\infty} \frac{\text{CF to firm}}{(1+K_O)^t}$$

where

V = Value of firm
CF = Future cash flows
$K_o$ = Discount rate.

Thus, the value of a firm can also be determined as under:

Value of firm = Present value of future cash flows during an explicit forecast period + Present value of cash flows after the explicit forecast period.

During the explicit forecast period, the firm is expected to evolve rather rapidly and hence a great deal of effort is extended to forecast its cash flow on an annual basis. At the end of the explicit forecast period the firm is expected to reach a study rate and hence a simplified procedure is used to estimate the continuing value as follows:

$$\text{Continuing Value} = \frac{FCFF_{T+1}}{K_o - g}$$

where

$FCFF_{T+1}$ is the unrealised level of free cash flow in the first year after the explicit forecast period.

$K_o$ = weighted average cost of capital

g = expected growth rate of free cash flow forever

## 3.4 OPERATING FREE CASH FLOWS

Operating free cash flow is the post-tax cash flow generated from the operations of the firm after providing for investments in fixed assets and net working capital required for the operations of the firm. The value of business prefer to discount expected future free cash flows to operating cash flows for the purpose of firm valuation. This is because firms are required to make investments in long-term assets as well as in working capital to generate future cash flows. Therefore, there is a need for adjusting operating cash flows to free cash flows.

The operating free cash flows are determined as follows:

After tax profit of the firm

*Add*: (1) Depreciation

(2) Non-cash expenditure

*Less*: (1) Income from marketable securities

(2) Extraordinary income

= Operating free cash flows.

The free cash flow is the legitimate cash flow for the purpose of business valuation because it reflects the cash flows generated by a company's operations for all the providers of its capital. The FCFF is a more comprehensive term as it includes cash flows due after tax non-operating income as well as adjustments for non-operating assets.

FCFF are available to all the capital providers of a company, the discount rate to be applied to such cash flows should be indicative of the opportunity cost of the funds made available by them, weighted by their relative contribution to the total capital of the company. The opportunity cost is equivalent to the rate of return, the investors expect to earn on other investments of equivalent risk. The cost to the company equals the investors cost less any tax benefits received by the company itself plus any tax payments required to be made. Thus, the value of the firm is equal to the present value of FCFF through infinity. The equity valuation can be determined by subtracting the total external liabilities from the value of the company.

A company's value depends on its free cash flow (FCF) which is defined as:

FCF = Net operating profit after tax – Net investment in operating capital

= NOPAT – Net investment in operating capital

= [EBIT × (1 – t)] – [Capital of the current year – Capital of the previous year.]

**Illustration 3.2:** The financial statements of Maruti Ltd. for the last 3 years are given below:

| **Profit Loss Account** | **(₹ lakhs)** | | |
|---|---|---|---|
| **Particulars** | **31.3.10** | **31.3.11** | **31.03.12** |
| Net sales | 180 | 200 | 229 |
| Income from interest | – | – | 03 |
| Non-operating income | – | – | 8 |
| Total income | 180 | 200 | 240 |
| Cost of goods sold | 100 | 120 | 125 |
| Adm. & S & D expenses | 30 | 35 | 45 |
| Deprecation | 12 | 15 | 18 |
| Interest expenses | 12 | 15 | 16 |
| Total cost | 154 | 170 | 204 |
| Profit before tax | 26 | 30 | 36 |
| Provision for tax | 8 | 9 | 12 |
| Profit after tax | 18 | 21 | 24 |
| Dividend | 11 | 12 | 12 |
| Retained earnings | 7 | 9 | 12 |

Rate of income tax is 30%

| **Balance Sheet** | (₹ lakhs) | | |
|---|---|---|---|
| **Particulars** | **31.03.10** | **31.3.11** | **31.3.12** |
| Equity Share Capital | 60 | 90 | 90 |
| Reserve and Surplus | 40 | 49 | 61 |
| Debt | 100 | 119 | 129 |
| Total | **200** | **258** | **280** |
| Fixed Assets | 150 | 175 | 190 |
| Investments | – | 20 | 20 |
| Net current Assets | 50 | 63 | 70 |
| Total | **200** | **258** | **280** |

You are required to determine the followings for the year ended 31.3.2012:

(a) EBIT

(b) Taxes on EBIT

(c) Net investment

(d) Free cash flow.

**Solution:**

(a) EBIT of Maruti Ltd. for the year ended 31.3.2012:

| | **(₹ lakhs)** |
|---|---|
| Profit before tax | 36 |
| + Interest expense | 16 |
| – Interest income | 3 |
| – Non-operating Income | 8 |
| EBIT | 41 |

(b) Taxes on EBIT for the year ended 31.3.2012:

| | **(₹ lakhs)** |
|---|---|
| Provision for tax | 12.00 |
| + Tax shield on interest expense | 4.80 |
| – Tax on interest income | 0.90 |
| – Tax on non-operating income | 2.40 |
| Tax on EBIT | 13.50 |

∴ Net operating profit after tax = ₹ 41 lakhs – ₹ 13.50 lakhs

= ₹ 27.50 lakhs

(c) Calculation of Net Investment for the year ended on 31.03.2012:

Net Investment = (Net Fixed Assets at the end of the year + Net current assets at the end of the year) – (Net fixed Assets at the beginning + Net current assets at the beginning)

= (₹ 190 lakhs + 70 lakhs) – (₹ 175 lakhs + 63 lakhs)

= ₹ 260 lakhs – 238 lakhs

= ₹ 22 lakhs.

(d) (i) Calculation of non-operating cash flow

= Non-operating Income × (1 – Tax Rate)

= ₹ 8 × (0.70) = ₹ 5.6 lakhs

(ii) Calculation of FCFF for the year ended 31.03.2012

= Nopat – Net Investment + Non-operating Cash Flow

= ₹ 27.50 – 22 + 5.6 lakhs

= ₹ 11.10 lakhs.

**Illustration 3.3:** Ajay Ltd. has employed a total capital of ₹ 100 lakh, provided equally by 10% debt and 5 lakh equity share of ₹ 10 each. Its cost of equity is 14 per cent and subject to corporate tax rate of 30 per cent. The projected free cash flows to all investors of the firm for next 5 years are given below:

| Year end | ₹ lakhs |
|---|---|
| 1 | 30 |
| 2 | 20 |
| 3 | 50 |
| 4 | 15 |
| 5 | 60 |

Compute (a) Valuation of firm

(b) Valuation from the perspective of equity shareholders.

Assume 10% debt is repayable at the end of 5[th] year and interest is paid at each year end.

**Solution:**

(a) (i) Computation of overall cost of capital

| Source | After Tax Cost | Weight | Total Cost % |
|---|---|---|---|
| Equity | 14 | 0.5 | 7.0 |
| Debt | 07 | 0.5 | 3.5 |
| Weighted average cost of capital | | | **10.50** |

$K_d = (10 - 30\%) = (10 - 3) = 7\%$

(ii) Valuation of firm based on $K_o$

| Year End | FCFF (₹ lakhs) | PV Factor 10% | Present Value (₹ lakhs) |
|---|---|---|---|
| 1 | 30 | 0.909 | 27.27 |
| 2 | 20 | 0.826 | 16.52 |
| 3 | 50 | 0.751 | 37.55 |
| 4 | 15 | 0.683 | 10.25 |
| 5 | 60 | 0.621 | 37.26 |
| Present value of firm | | | 128.85 |
| – Value of debt | | | 50.00 |
| Value of equity | | | **78.85** |

(b) Valuation of Equity based on $K_e$

| Year End | FCFF to All Investor | After Tax Payment to Debenture Holder | FCFE to Equity Shareholder | P.V. Factor @10% | Present Value (₹ lakhs) |
|---|---|---|---|---|---|
| 1 | 30 | 3.5 | 26.5 | 0.877 | 23.24 |
| 2 | 20 | 3.5 | 16.5 | 0.769 | 12.69 |
| 3 | 50 | 3.5 | 46.5 | 0.675 | 31.39 |
| 4 | 15 | 3.5 | 11.5 | 0.592 | 6.81 |
| 5 | 60 | 53.5 | 6.5 | 0.519 | 3.37 |
| Present value of Equity | | | | | **77.50** |

Interest on 50 lakh @10% = ₹ 5 lakh

∴ 5 lakh (1 – t) = 5(0.7) = ₹ 3.5 lakh

**Illustration 3.4:** Pritam Ltd. is expected to generally the following free cash flow cover the next 5 years:

| Year | Free Cash Flow |
|---|---|
| 2007-08 | 2,50,000 |
| 2008-09 | 2,90,000 |
| 2009-10 | 3,20,000 |
| 2010-11 | 3,60,000 |
| 2011.12 | 4,00,000 |

The company is expected to show a constant growth of 4% after 200 11.12. If the cost of equity is 12%, what is the value of the firm?

**Solution:**

(i) $\text{Terminal value in 2011.12} = \dfrac{\text{FCFE}}{r-g}$

where

FCFE = Free cash flow at the end of year 2011-12

r = cost of equity

g = growth rate in cash flow

$$\therefore TV = \frac{4{,}00{,}000\,(1.04)}{0.12-0.04} = ₹\,\frac{4{,}16{,}000}{0.08}$$

$$= ₹\,52{,}00{,}000$$

∴ Value of firm

| Year | FCFFY (₹) | D.F. @12% | P.V. (₹) |
|---|---|---|---|
| 2007-8 | 2,50,000 | 0.893 | 2,23,250 |
| 2008-9 | 2,90,000 | 0.797 | 2,31,130 |
| 2009-10 | 3,20,000 | 0.712 | 2,27,840 |
| 2010-11 | 3,60,000 | 0.636 | 2,28,960 |
| 2011-12 | 4,00,000 | 0.567 | 2,26,800 |
| 2011-12 | 52,00,000 (TV) | 0.567 | 29,48,400 |
| Value of firm | | | **40,86,380** |

**Illustration 3.5:** Sajan Industries deals in production and sales of consumer durables. It is expecting sales revenues for the next 8 years as follows:

| Year | Sales Revenue (₹ lakhs) |
|---|---|
| 1 | 80 |
| 2 | 100 |
| 3 | 150 |
| 4 | 220 |
| 5 | 300 |
| 6 | 260 |
| 7 | 230 |
| 8 | 200 |

Its condensed Balance sheet as on 31st March, 2012 is as follows:

| Liabilities | ₹ lakhs | Assets | ₹ lakhs |
|---|---|---|---|
| Equity Funds | 120 | Fixed Assets | 170 |
| 12% Debt | 80 | Current Assets (net) | 30 |
| | **200** | | **200** |

**Additional Information:**

(i) Its variable expenses will amount to 40 per cent of sales revenue. Fixed cash operating costs are estimated to be ₹ 16 lakhs per year for the first 4 years and at ₹ 20 lakhs for 5th to 8th year. In addition an extensive advertisement campaign will be launched, requiring annual outlays as follows:

| Year | ₹ lakhs |
|---|---|
| 1 | 5 |
| 2-3 | 15 |
| 4-6 | 30 |
| 7-8 | 10 |

(ii) Fixed assets are subject to depreciation at 15 per cent p.a., on WDV methods.

(iii) The company has planned the following capital expenditure for the next 8 years to be incurred at the beginning of each year:

| Year | ₹ lakhs |
|---|---|
| 1 | 5 |
| 2 | 8 |
| 3 | 20 |
| 4 | 25 |
| 5 | 35 |
| 6 | 25 |
| 7 | 15 |
| 8 | 10 |

(iv) Working capital in terms of investment in current assets are estimated at 20 per cent of the sales revenue.

(v) It is expected to have non-operating assets in terms of investments in marketable securities in the initial year. The expected after tax non-operating cash flow in the first year is ₹ 50,000.

(vi) The effective tax rate is 30 per cent.

(vii) The cost of equity is at 16%.

(viii) The free cash flow of the firm are expected to grow at 5 per cent per annum after 8th year.

You are requested to determine the discounted cash flow value of the company.

**Solution:**

(a) Calculation of Weighted Average Cost of Capital

| **Source** | **Cost** | **Weight** | **Total (%)** |
|---|---|---|---|
| Equity | 16 | 0.6 | 9.60 |
| Debt | 8.4 | 0.4 | 3.36 |
| | | | **12.96** |

(b) Calculation of Depreciation

| **Year** | **Cost ₹ lakhs** | **Additions ₹ lakhs** | **Total ₹ lakhs** | **Depreciation ₹ lakhs** |
|---|---|---|---|---|
| 1 | 170 | 5 | 175 | 26.25 |
| 2 | 148.75 | 8 | 156.75 | 23.51 |
| 3 | 133.24 | 20 | 153.24 | 22.99 |
| 4 | 130.25 | 25 | 155.25 | 23.29 |
| 5 | 131.96 | 35 | 166.96 | 25.04 |
| 6 | 141.92 | 25 | 166.92 | 25.04 |
| 7 | 141.88 | 15 | 156.88 | 23.53 |
| 8 | 133.35 | 10 | 143.35 | 21.5 |

(c) Calculation of Additional Investment Required

| **Year** | **Capital Expenditure ₹ lakhs** | **Working Capital ₹ lakhs (20% of Sales)** | **Total ₹ lakhs** | **Existing Investment ₹ lakhs** | **Additional Investment ₹ lakhs** |
|---|---|---|---|---|---|
| 1 | 5 | 16 | 21 | 30 | Nil |
| 2 | 8 | 20 | 28 | 25 | 3 |
| 3 | 20 | 30 | 50 | 20 | 30 |
| 4 | 25 | 44 | 69 | 30 | 39 |
| 5 | 35 | 60 | 95 | 44 | 51 |
| 6 | 25 | 52 | 77 | 60 | 17 |
| 7 | 15 | 46 | 61 | 52 | 9 |
| 8 | 10 | 40 | 50 | 46 | 4 |

(d) Calculation of Present Value for Explicit Period Projection

**₹ in lakhs**

| **Particular** | **1** | **2** | **3** | **4** | **5** | **6** | **7** | **8** |
|---|---|---|---|---|---|---|---|---|
| Sales revenue | 80 | 100 | 150 | 220 | 300 | 260 | 230 | 200 |
| *Less*: Expenses /variable cost | 32 | 40 | 60 | 88 | 120 | 104 | 92 | 80 |
| Fixed cost/operating cost | 16 | 16 | 16 | 16 | 20 | 20 | 20 | 20 |
| Advertisement | 5 | 15 | 15 | 30 | 30 | 30 | 10 | 10 |
| Depreciation | 26.25 | 23.51 | 22.99 | 23.29 | 25.04 | 25.04 | 23.53 | 21.5 |
| EBIT | 0.75 | 5.49 | 36.01 | 62.71 | 104.96 | 80.96 | 84.47 | 68.5 |
| – Taxes | 0.22 | 1.65 | 10.8 | 18.81 | 31.49 | 24.29 | 25.34 | 20.55 |
| NOPAT | 0.53 | 3.84 | 25.21 | 43.9 | 73.47 | 56.67 | 59.13 | 47.95 |
| Non operating income | 0.5 | | | | | | | |
| Gross cash flow including depreciation | 27.28 | 27.35 | 48.2 | 67.19 | 98.51 | 81.71 | 82.66 | 69.45 |
| *Less*: Investments | – | 3 | 30 | 39 | 51 | 17 | 9 | 4 |
| Free cash flow | 27.28 | 24.35 | 18.2 | 28.19 | 47.51 | 64.71 | 73.66 | 65.45 |
| Discounting factor @13% | 0.89 | 0.78 | 0.69 | 0.61 | 0.54 | 0.48 | 0.25 | 0.38 |
| Present value | 24.14 | 19.07 | 12.61 | 17.28 | 25.8 | 31.06 | 31.31 | 24.61 |

Total present value = ₹ 185.88 lakhs.

(e) Calculation of continuing value

$$CV_8 = \frac{FCFg}{K_o - g} = \frac{65.45(1.05)}{(0.13 - 0.05)}$$

$$= \frac{68.72}{0.08} = ₹859 \text{ lakhs}$$

∴ Present Value of CV = ₹ 859 × 0.376

= ₹ 322.98 lakhs.

(f) Value of firm = P.V. of free cash flows during explicit period
+ P.V. of free cash flows after explicit period
= ₹ 185.88 lakhs + 322.98 lakhs
= ₹ 508.86 lakhs.

**Illustration 3.6:** From the following information determine continuing value of 'M' Ltd.

| | |
|---|---|
| Cash flow from business operations at the end of explicit forecast period (5 years) | ₹ 20 lakhs |
| Investment in current assets required in 5 years | ₹ 2 lakhs |
| Expected annual growth rate in free cash flows after forecast period (%) | 5% |
| Weighted average cost of capital | 12% |
| Cost of debt | 8% |

**Solution:**

(a) Continuing value $= \dfrac{FCFF_6}{K_o - g} = \dfrac{20-2}{12\% - 5\%}$

$$CV_5 = \frac{18\,(1.05)}{0.12 - 0.05}$$

$$= \frac{18.90}{0.07} = ₹\ 270 \text{ lakhs}$$

(b) $CV_o$ = P.V. factor @12% for 5 years × 270

= 0.567 × 270

= ₹ 155.09 lakhs

**Illustration 3.7:** The following data are related to Mohan Ltd. as on 31st March, 2012:

| | |
|---|---|
| Free cash flows from business operations at the end of explicit forecast period (9 years) | ₹ 176 lakhs |
| Growth rate in free cash flows | 10% p.a. |
| Weighted average cost of capital | 14% |

Determine the continuing value of the firm.

**Solution:**

$$\text{Continuing value at the end of } 8^{th} \text{ year} = \frac{\text{FCFF at the end of 9 years}}{K_o - g}$$

$$= \frac{176}{14\% - 10\%}$$

$$= \frac{176}{0.14 - 0.10}$$

$$= \frac{176}{0.04} = ₹\ 440 \text{ lakhs.}$$

**Illustration 3.8:** The following data are related to MIRC Ltd.

| | (₹ lakhs) | | | | |
|---|---|---|---|---|---|
| **Particulars** | **2007** | **2008** | **2009** | **2010** | **2011** |
| Net sales | 10,000 | 11,550 | 13,340 | 15,408 | 17,796 |
| EBITDA | 2,000 | 2,310 | 2,668 | 3,082 | 3,559 |
| Depreciation | 500 | 577 | 667 | 770 | 890 |
| EBIT | 1,500 | 1,733 | 2,001 | 2,312 | 2,669 |
| Interest | 300 | 346 | 400 | 462 | 534 |
| EBT | 1,200 | 1,387 | 1,601 | 1,850 | 2,135 |
| Tax @40% | 480 | 555 | 640 | 740 | 854 |
| Net income | 720 | 832 | 961 | 1,110 | 1,281 |
| Capital expenditure | 900 | 1,039 | 1,201 | 1,387 | 1,602 |
| Increase in working capital | 400 | 462 | 534 | 616 | 712 |
| Discount factor @10% | 0.9 | 0.83 | 0.75 | 0.68 | 0.62 |

You are required to determine the value of firm using discounted Cash Flow Techniques assuming terminal period discount rate of 12%.

**Solution:**

(a) DCF Valuation Approach

| | (₹ lakhs) | | | | |
|---|---|---|---|---|---|
| **Particulars** | **2007** | **2008** | **2009** | **2010** | **2011** |
| Sales | 10,000 | 11,550 | 13,340 | 15,408 | 17,796 |
| EBITDA | 2,000 | 2,310 | 2,668 | 3,082 | 3,559 |
| Deprecation | 500 | 577 | 667 | 770 | 890 |
| EBIT | 1,500 | 1,733 | 2,001 | 2,312 | 2,669 |
| Interest | 300 | 346 | 400 | 462 | 534 |
| EBT | 1,200 | 1,387 | 1,601 | 1,850 | 2,135 |
| Tax @40% | 480 | 555 | 640 | 740 | 854 |
| Net income | 720 | 832 | 961 | 1,110 | 1,281 |
| Add interest saved | 180 | 208 | 240 | 277 | 320 |
| NOPAT | 900 | 1,040 | 1,201 | 1,387 | 1,602 |
| + Depreciation | 500 | 577 | 667 | 770 | 890 |
| – Capital exp. | 900 | 1,039 | 1,201 | 1,387 | 1,602 |
| – Working capital | 400 | 462 | 534 | 616 | 712 |
| Free cash flow | 100 | 116 | 133 | 154 | 177 |
| D.F. @10% | 0.91 | 0.83 | 0.75 | 0.68 | 0.62 |
| Present value | 91 | 96 | 100 | 105 | 110 |

Total present value = 91 + 96 + 100 + 105 + 110 = ₹ 502 lakhs

(b) DCF Valuation for Terminal Period

| | |
|---|---|
| EBITDA for 2012 | ₹ 3,559 lakhs |
| Free cash flow in 2012 | ₹ 1,601 lakhs |
| Terminal period discount rate | 12% |
| ∴ Terminal value in 2012 (1,601 ÷ 12%) | ₹ 13,345 lakhs |
| Present value factor @12% | 0.6209 |
| ∴ Present value of Terminal Period (13,345 × 0.6209) | ₹ 8,286 lakhs |

(c) Value of firm = ₹ 502 + 8,286

= ₹ 8,788 lakhs.

**Illustration 3.9:** Wax Ltd. has estimated the free cash flows for the next five years as under:

| Year | Free cash flow (₹ lakhs) |
|---|---|
| 1 | 3.0 |
| 2 | 5.8 |
| 3 | 16.6 |
| 4 | 13.8 |
| 5 | 16.0 |

The free cash flow will grow at the rate of 10% from 6th year. The cost of capital is 14%. The value of non-operating assets (excess marketable securities) is ₹ 20 lakhs. You are required to determine the value of the firm.

**Solution:**

Value of firm = Present value of future cash flows
+ Present value of continuing valuation
+ Value of non-operating assets.

(a) Present value of further cash flows

| Year | Cash Flow (₹ lakhs) | D.F. @14% | Present Value (₹ lakhs) |
|---|---|---|---|
| 1 | 3 | 0.877 | 2.631 |
| 2 | 5.8 | 0.769 | 4.460 |
| 3 | 16.6 | 0.675 | 11.205 |
| 4 | 13.8 | 0.592 | 8.170 |
| 5 | 16.0 | 0.519 | 8.304 |
| Total | | | **34.77** |

(b) Continuing value $= \dfrac{FCFF_6}{K_o - g}$

$FCFF_6$ = FCFF at 5th year + 10%
= 16 + 1.6 = ₹ 17.6 lakhs

$$\therefore CV_6 = \frac{17.6}{14 - 10\%} = \frac{17.6}{0.14 - 0.10}$$

$$= \frac{17.6}{0.04} = ₹\ 44 \text{ lakhs}$$

Present value of CV = $44 \times 0.519$
= ₹ 22.84 lakhs

(c) Value of non-operating assets = ₹ 20 lakhs

(d) Value of firm = 34.77 + ₹ 22.84 + ₹ 20 lakhs
= ₹ 77.61 lakhs

**Illustration 3.10:** The finance manager of Raymonds Ltd. has estimated the future free cash flows as follows:

| Year | Free Cash Flows (₹ lakhs) |
|---|---|
| 1 | 22 |
| 2 | 23 |
| 3 | 25 |
| 4 | 26 |
| 5 | 30 |
| 6 | 32 |

Free cash flows in subsequent years are estimated to grow at 4 per cent. The company's weighted average cost of capital is 12 per cent. The external liabilities are amounted to ₹ 36 lakhs and the company had issued one lakh equity shares.

You are required to calculate:

(a) Value of firm

(b) Value per share.

**Solution:**

(a) Calculation of present value of FCFE

(₹ lakhs)

| Year | FCFF | P.V. Factor@12% | Present Value |
|---|---|---|---|
| 1 | 22 | 0.893 | 19.646 |
| 2 | 23 | 0.797 | 18.331 |
| 3 | 25 | 0.712 | 17.44 |
| 4 | 26 | 0.636 | 16.536 |
| 5 | 30 | 0.567 | 17.010 |
| 6 | 32 | 0.507 | 16.224 |
| Total Present value | | | **105.19** |

(b) Present value of FCFF subsequent to explicit forecast period

$$CV_6 = \frac{FCFF(1+g)}{WACC - g}$$

$$= \frac{32\,(1.04)}{0.12 - 0.04} = \frac{33.28}{0.08} = ₹\,416 \text{ lakhs}$$

∴ Present value of $CV_6$ = ₹ 416 × 0.507 lakhs

= ₹ 210.912 lakhs

(c) Present value of firm = PV of FCFF + PV of $FCFF_6$

= ₹ 105.191 lakhs + 210.912 lakhs

= ₹ 316.103 lakhs

(d) Valuation per share = Value of firm – External liabilities

= ₹ 316.103 lakhs – ₹ 36.000 lakhs

= ₹ 280.103 lakhs

$$\therefore \text{Value per share} = \frac{280.103}{1{,}00{,}000} = ₹\,280.$$

## 3.5 EXERCISES

1. What is discounted cash flow approach? How are the firms valued on the basis of this approach?
2. What is cash flow? How are future cash flows estimated?
3. What is continuing value? How is it determined?
4. What is the major difference between the firm's free cash flow and free cash flow for equity?
5. What is free cash flow of the firm? What are its components?
6. "The discounted cash flow approach is conceptually the most ideal among various approaches for business valuation". Explain.
7. Write short notes on:
   (a) Continuing value
   (b) Free cash flow
   (c) Operating free cash flows
   (d) Weighted average cost of capital
   (e) Non-operating cash flow.
8. The finance manager of mega fast food chain has estimated future free cash flows of the company for 6 years as follows.

| Year End | Free Cash Flow ₹ lakhs |
|---|---|
| 1 | 400 |
| 2 | 800 |
| 3 | 1,050 |
| 4 | 1,400 |
| 5 | 950 |
| 6 | 600 |

The FCFF are expected to be constant at 18,600 lakhs after 6 year. You are required to compute the value of the firm assuming 13% cost of capital.

(Answer: 5,585.38 lakhs)

9. Determine the continuing value of 'C' Ltd. from the following information.

| | ₹ lakhs |
|---|---|
| Cash flow from business operations at the end of the explicit forecast period (5 years) | 2,000 |
| Investment in current Assets required in 5 years | 200 |
| Expected Annual growth rate in force cash flows | 5% |
| Weighted average cost of capital | 12% |
| Cost of Debt | 8% |

(Answer: ₹ 26,791 lakhs)

10. The Profit and Loss account and Balance Sheet of Nirmal Ltd. for two years are given below:

| **(a) Profit Loss Account** | **₹ lakhs** | |
|---|---|---|
| | **2011** | **2012** |
| Net sales | 56,000 | 64,400 |
| Income from marketable securities | 1,400 | 2,100 |
| Non-operating income | 700 | 1,400 |
| Total income | 58,100 | 67,900 |
| Cost of goods sold | 32,200 | 37,800 |
| Selling and Adm. expenses | 7,000 | 7,700 |
| Depreciation | 3,500 | 4,200 |
| Interest expenses | 3,360 | 3,920 |
| Total cost | 46,060 | 53,620 |
| EBT | 12,040 | 14,280 |
| – Tax | 3,640 | 4,480 |
| PAT | 8,400 | 9,800 |
| **(b) Balance Sheet** | | |
| Equity capital | 21,000 | 21,000 |
| Reserve and Surplus | 16,800 | 21,000 |
| Debt | 25,200 | 29,400 |
| | **63,000** | **71,400** |
| Fixed assets | 42,000 | 45,500 |
| Investments | 12,600 | 14,000 |
| Net current assets | 8,400 | 11,900 |
| | **63,000** | **71,400** |

You are required to determine the free cash flow for the firm for the year 2012.
(Answer: ₹ 3,892 lakhs)

11. The projected free cash flow of X Ltd. for year 7 is ₹ 11,780 lakhs. Thereafter it is expected to growth at a constant rate of 14 per cent per annum. The weighted average cost of capital is 17%. Determine the expected continuing value at the end of 7th year.
(Answer: ₹ 4,47,640 lakhs)

12. The data relating to Extra Ltd. is given as under:

| **Year** | **1** | **2** | **3** | **4** | **5** |
|---|---|---|---|---|---|
| Profit after tax | 29 | 28 | 32 | 38 | 40 |
| Fixed assets | 220 | 240 | 266 | 294 | 324 |
| Investments | 10 | – | – | – | – |
| Net current assets | 75 | 88 | 90 | 100 | 109 |
| Debt | 140 | 150 | 161 | 177 | 192 |

The FCFE forecast for the explicit forecast period is worked out as under:

| | 1 | 2 | 3 | 4 | 5 |
|---|---|---|---|---|---|
| PAT | 29 | 28 | 32 | 38 | 40 |
| Capital expenditure and depreciation | 30 | 20 | 26 | 28 | 30 |
| Change in current assets | 5 | 13 | 2 | 10 | 9 |
| New debt - Debt repayment | 11 | 10 | 11 | 16 | 15 |
| Change in investment in marketable securities | 10 | 10 | – | – | – |
| FCFE | 15 | 15 | 15 | 16 | 16 |

The company aspects that the FCFE grows at a constant rate of 10 per cent per year after the explicit period.

You are required to find out the value of equity of the firm assuming WACC @18%.

(Answer: ₹ 1,395 lakhs)

# Chapter 4 RELATIVE VALUATION

4.1 Introduction
4.2 Relative Valuation Approach
4.3 PEG Ratios
4.4 EV/EBIT Multiples
4.5 Price/Book Value Ratios
4.6 Sales Multiples
4.7 Choosing the Right Multiple
4.8 Exercises

## 4.1 INTRODUCTION

Value maximization is the central theme in financial management of any business organisation. In the wake of economic liberalisation companies are relying more on the capital market. Acquisitions and restructuring are becoming commonplace. Strategic alliances are gaining popularity. Under these circumstances the valuation of a company has become a crucial exercise. The goal of such an exercise is to estimate fair market value of a company. The fair market value is the value or price at which the property would change hands between a utility buyer and a willing seller and both the parties are having reasonable knowledge of relevant facts. There are various approaches for appraising the value of a company. Some of the approaches are Book value approach, Earning approach, Net assets value approach and Discounted cash flow approach. There is one more approach to valuation and that is, Relative valuation approach.

The common sense and economic logic tells us that similar assets should sell at similar prices. Based on this principle, we can value an asset by looking at the price at which a comparable asset has changed hands between a reasonably informed seller. This approach is commonly applied in real estates. If there are two identical or near-identical apartments or business their values should normally be similar. If two companies are changed in the similar business line, then their valuation should also be made on similar basis.

## 4.2 RELATIVE VALUATION APPROACH

The relative valuation apply a relation of specific financial or operations characteristics from a similar company or industry. The relative valuations express the value of company as a multiple of a specific static or parameter. However, in case the base for valuation is wrong, the valuation of the company can also go wrong. The value of business can be determined on the basis of certain operational characteristics such as Divisional yield, Earnings yield, Return on capital employed and Price-earning relative. The following valuation models are generally used based on the industry averages or averages of a similar company in the same industry.

## (a) Price-earning Relative

Price-earning Ratio is the relation between market price of a share and earning per share of a company. The price-earning ratio can be determined as follows:

$$\text{P/E Ratio} = \frac{\text{Market Price per Share}}{\text{Earnings per Share}}.$$

The market price per share is taken from the Stock Exchange quotations for a particular date or average market price of the share in the stock market. The earning per equity share is calculated as follows:

$$\text{EPS} = \frac{\text{PAT} - \text{Preference Dividend}}{\text{No. of Equity Shares}}.$$

PAT = Profit after Tax, which is taken from profit & loss account.

The value per share can be determined as follows:

Value per Share = Earning per Share × P/E Ratio.

The P/E ratio can be used as a valuation of shares and business. This ratio is expressed as a number. It can be seen as the number of years the investor should wait to recover the invested amount out of earnings on the investment in shares. The dividend may be distributed or may not be. However, dividend is related to the profit of the company. The P/E ratio can be used when it is not realistic to estimate the yearly cash flows into the future. Financial analysis often use P/E Ratio as a guide to the market value. Listed companies offer significant advantages to their members as their shares are marketable. Their large size gives them an element of stability and it makes their shares more desirable. They are highly priced in the market as compared to the unlisted companies. The value of business can be determined as follows:

Value of Business = Market Price per Share × No. of Equity Share

OR

= Company's expected future maintainable profits × Industry Average P/E Ratio.

**Illustration 4.1:** Prabhat Ltd. is having an issued and subscribed capital of 50 lakh equity shares of ₹ 10 each fully paid-up. The company's after tax profits for the year 2011 is amounting to ₹ 280 lakhs. The average present stock exchange price of the company's share is ₹ 22.40. The price-earning ratios of the four listed companies engaged in similar businesses are given below:

| Company | 2009 | 2010 | 2011 |
|---|---|---|---|
| A Ltd. | 5.7 | 6.3 | 7.1 |
| B Ltd. | 5.9 | 6.5 | 6.8 |
| C Ltd. | 6.8 | 7.0 | 7.4 |
| D Ltd. | 5.0 | 5.9 | 6.1 |

You are required to calculate the value of business and value per share based on average P/E ratio of the Industry.

**Solution:**

(a) Calculation of Average P/E Ratio of Industry

| Company | 2009 | 2010 | 2011 | Average |
|---|---|---|---|---|
| A Ltd. | 5.7 | 6.3 | 7.1 | 6.37 |
| B Ltd. | 5.9 | 6.5 | 6.8 | 6.40 |
| C Ltd. | 6.8 | 7.0 | 7.4 | 7.07 |
| D Ltd. | 5.0 | 5.9 | 6.1 | 5.67 |
| Total | | | | **25.51** |

$$\text{Industry Average P/E Ratio} = \frac{25.51}{4} = 6.38 \text{ Times}$$

(b) Calculation of Expected Earning per Share of Prabhat Ltd. $= \dfrac{\text{Profit After Tax}}{\text{No. of Equity Shares}}$

$$= \frac{₹\,280 \text{ lakhs}}{50 \text{ lakhs}}$$

$$= ₹\,5.6$$

(c) Calculation of Company P/E Ratio $= \dfrac{\text{Market Price per Share}}{\text{Earnings per Share}}$

$$= \frac{22.40}{5.6} = 4 \text{ Times}$$

(d) Value of Business = Company's Expected Future Maintainable Profit × Industry Average P/E Ratio

$= ₹$ 280 lakhs × 6.38

$= ₹$ 1,286.4 lakhs

(e) Value per Share = EPS × P/E Ratio

$= ₹\,5.6 \times 6.38$

$= ₹$ 35.73

**Illustration 4.2:** Pritam Industries Ltd. is having an issued and subscribed capital of ₹ 50 lakh equity shares of ₹ 10 each fully paid up. The company's after tax profits for the year ended 2011 was ₹ 320 lakhs. The average Stock Exchange price of the Company's share is ₹ 23. The P/E ratio of the industry is 8 times. You are required to calculate the value of a share and value of business based on average P/E ratio of the industry.

**Solution:**

(a) Expected Earnings per Share of Pritam Ltd. $= \dfrac{\text{Profit After Tax}}{\text{No. of Equity Shares}}$

$$= \frac{320}{50} = ₹\,6.40$$

(b) Calculation of Company's P/E Ratio $= \dfrac{\text{Market Price per Share}}{\text{Earning per Share}}$

$$= ₹\frac{23}{6.4} = 3.6 \text{ Times}$$

(c) Valuation of Company's Share = EPS × P/E Ratio of Industry

= ₹ 6.40 × 8

= ₹ 51.20

(d) Value of Business = Company's Expected Future Maintainable Profit × Industry P/E Ratio

= ₹ 320 × 8 lakhs

= ₹ 2,560 lakhs

OR

Value of Business = Market Price × No. of Shares Issued

= ₹ 51.20 × 50 lakhs

= ₹ 2,560 lakhs

**Illustration 4.3:** Centre Ltd., has one lakh, 11% preference share of ₹ 100 each fully paid up, and 40 lakh equity shares of ₹ 10 each fully paid-up. The P/E Ratio of the company is 8 times. The company has reported a profit of ₹ 65 lakhs, after paying taxes @35 per cent. However, the current years income includes (i) extraordinary income of ₹ 10 lakh and (ii) extraordinary loss of ₹ 3 lakh. Apart from existing operations, which are normal in nature, and are likely to continue in future, the company expects to a launch a new product in the coming year. The revenue and cost estimates in respect of the new product are as follows:

| | **₹ lakhs** |
|---|---|
| Sales | 60 |
| Material cost | 15 |
| Labour cost | 10 |
| Allocated fixed cost | 5 |
| Additional fixed cost | 8 |

You are required to calculate the value of the business using P/E Ratio.

**Solution:**

(a) Calculation of Earning per Share

| **Future Maintainable Profit** | **₹ lakhs** |
|---|---|
| Profit before tax (₹ 65 /(1–0.35)) | 100 |
| *Less*: Extraordinary income | 10 |
| *Add*: Extraordinary loss | 3 |
| *Add*: Incremental income (60–15–10–8) | 27 |
| Expected profit before tax | **120** |
| *Less*: Taxes @35% | 42 |
| Future maintainable profit | **78** |

$$\text{EPS} = \frac{\text{PAT} - \text{Pref. Dividend}}{\text{No. of Eq. Shares}}$$

$$= \frac{78 - 11}{40} = \frac{77}{40} = ₹1.675$$

(b) Calculation of Market Price per Share

$$\text{P/E Ratio} = \frac{\text{Market Price per Share}}{\text{EPS}}$$

$$8 \text{ Times} = \frac{\text{M.P.}}{1.675}$$

$$\therefore \text{M.P.} = 8 \times 1.675 = ₹13.40$$

(c) Value of Business = M.P. per Share × No. of Eq. Shares

= 13.40 × 40

= 536 lakhs

## (b) Earnings Yield Approach

The value of a company on the earning yield basis is the value of the stream of profits or earnings which the company is expected to generate. The earnings of the company belongs to the shareholders whether distributed or not, as dividend. The undistributed profit is used to finance the growth of the business. It also helps to increase the value of share. The value of business can be determined as follows:

(a) To predict the future maintainable profit of the company

(b) Identify the required earnings yield by reference to the results of similar companies

(c) Apply the earnings yield to future profit using the following formula:

$$\text{Value of Business} = \frac{\text{Company's expected future maintainable profit}}{\text{Industry normal earning yield}}$$

The profit figure can be taken from the profit and loss account of the company. However, factors which cause distortions and changes anticipated in the future should be taken into account while estimating the future earnings.

**Illustration 4.4:** 'H' Ltd. agrees to acquire 'K' Ltd. based on the capitalization of last three years profits of 'K' Ltd. at an earnings yield of 20% profits of 'K' Ltd. are given below:

| Year | Profit (₹ lakhs) |
|---|---|
| 2009 | 70 |
| 2010 | 90 |
| 2011 | 80 |

Calculate the value of business on the earnings yield basis.

**Solution:**

(a) Average profit of 'K' Ltd. = $\frac{70 + 90 + 80}{3} = \frac{240}{3} = ₹80$ lakhs

(b) Earning yield is 20%

(c) Value of Business = $\frac{\text{Average Profit}}{\text{Earnings Yield}} = \frac{80}{0.20} = ₹\ 400$ lakhs.

**Illustration 4.5:** The balance sheet of Sunshine Ltd. as on 31st March, 2012 was as follows:

| Liabilities | ₹ lakh | Assets | ₹ lakh |
|---|---|---|---|
| Equity share capital (₹ 10 each) | 40 | Goodwill | 4 |
| Reserves and Surplus | 9 | Fixed Assets | 50 |
| Profit loss account | 2 | Current Assets | 20 |
| 10% Debentures | 10 | | |
| Current liabilities | 13 | | |
| | **74** | | **74** |

On 31st March, 2012, the goodwill of the company was revalued at ₹ 5,00,000 while other fixed assets where valued at ₹ 35 lakhs. The net profit earned by the company amounted to ₹ 52 lakhs for the year 2009-10, ₹ 51 lakhs for the year 2010-11 and ₹ 53 lakhs for the year 2011-12. Every year an amount of 20% of the net profit earned was transferred to general reserves. A return of 12.5 per cent on investment is considered fair in the industry. Compute the value of the company using earnings yield method.

**Solution:**

(i) Calculation of Expected Average Profits

| Year | Profit (₹ lakhs) |
|---|---|
| 2009-10 | 52 |
| 2010-11 | 51 |
| 2011-12 | 53 |
| Total | **156** |

$$\therefore \text{Average profit} = \frac{156}{3} = ₹\ 52 \text{ lakhs}$$

(ii) Calculation of Balance of Profit

| | |
|---|---|
| Average profit | ₹ 52.00 lakhs |
| *Less*: Transfer to Reserve | ₹ 10.40 lakhs |
| Net profit | 41.60 lakhs |

(iii) Calculation of Rate of Return = $\frac{\text{Expected Profit}}{\text{Equity Yield}} = \frac{41.6}{40} \times 100 = 104\%$

(iv) Calculation of Value per Share = $\frac{\text{Rate of Return}}{\text{Normal Rate}} \times \text{Paid - up Value for Share}$

$$= \frac{104}{12.5} \times 100 = ₹\ 83.20$$

(v) Value of Business = Value per Share × No. of Equity Shares

= 83.20 × 4

= ₹ 332.8 lakhs

**Illustration 4.6:** The following details are given relating to X Ltd. for the year end of 31st March, 2012.

| | ₹ lakhs |
|---|---|
| 20,000, 9% Preference share of ₹ 100 each | 20 |
| 5,00,000 Equity shares of ₹ 10 each, ₹ 8 per share paid up | 40 |
| Expected profit per year before tax | 220 |
| Rate of tax | 30% |
| Transfer to general reserves 20% of net profit | |
| Normal rate of earnings | 15% |

Calculated the value of business as well as value per equity share of the company.

**Solution:**

(i) Calculation of profit available to Equity Holders

| | ₹ lakhs |
|---|---|
| Expected profit before tax | 220.00 |
| *Less*: Tax | 66.00 |
| Profit after tax | 154.00 |
| *Less*: Transfer to reserve 20 % | 30.80 |
| Profit after tax reserve | 123.20 |
| *Less*: Preference dividend | 1.80 |
| Profit available to equity shareholders | 121.40 |

(ii) Calculation of Expected Rate of Earnings $= \dfrac{\text{Profit Available to Equity Holders}}{\text{Equity Share Capital}} \times 100$

$$= \frac{121.40}{40} \times 100 = 30.35\%$$

(iii) Calculation of Value of Equity Share

$$\text{Value per Share} = \frac{\text{Expected Return}}{\text{Normal Rate}} \times \text{Paid - up Value}$$

$$= \frac{30.35}{15} \times 8 = ₹\,17.18$$

(iv) Value of Equity = 17.18 × 5,00,000

= ₹ 85.90 lakhs

(v) Value of Business = Value of Equity + Value of Preference Share

= ₹ 85.90 lakhs + 20 lakhs

= ₹ 105.90 lakhs

## (c) Dividend Yield Approach

The ownership in the shares of a company entails the holder to receive dividends as and when declared by the company. The investor in a company get their return in the form of dividend, the amount of dividend paid gives some indication of how valuable the shares will be to the potential buyer. While valuing a small shareholding, the calculation should be based on the dividends rather than earnings per share. Therefore, the relationship between the level of dividend and price in other companies and base a price on what dividend is normally paid.

The dividend policy of a company determines the portion of earnings to be paid to the shareholders by way of dividends and the portion to be ploughed back in the form of reinvestment purposes. The dividends policy has a bearing on the choice of financing. A firm's dividend payout ratio obviously depends on how earnings are measured. However, accounting earnings often diverge from economic earnings and do not truly reflect a firm's capacity to pay dividends. As the principal objective of corporate financial management is to maximize the market value of equity shares, it is important to determine relation between dividend policy and market price of equity shares. The value of shares and the firm can be determined as follows:

$$\text{Value per Share} = \frac{\text{Dividend per Share}}{\text{Industry Average Dividend per Share}} \times \text{Face Value per Share}$$

OR

$$\text{Value per Share} = \frac{\text{Rate of Dividend}}{\text{Industry Normal Rate of Dividend}} \times \text{Face Value per Share}$$

Value of Business = Value per Equity Share × Number of Equity Share

The dividend yield method had certain limitations. It ignores the element of capital gain which is the important financial justification for investing in shares. The growth of a company could be seen as a means to secure the flow of dividends to the shareholders in future rather than a goal in itself. The approach is based on the assumption that dividend policy will remain constant. In practice the companies change their dividend policies from time to time.

**Illustration 4.7:** Ambica Builders has an issued and paid-up capital of 5 lakh shares of ₹ 10 each. The company declared a dividend of ₹ 12.5 lakhs during the last five years and expects to maintain the same level of dividends in future. The control and ownership of the company is lying in few hands of directors and their family members. The average dividend yield for listed companies in the same line of business is 12.5%. You are required to determine the value of business using the concept of dividend yield.

**Solution:**

(a) Average Dividend Declared per Share $= \frac{\text{Dividend}}{\text{No. of Share}} = \frac{12.50}{5} = ₹\ 2.50$

(b) Value per Share $= \frac{\text{Co's Dividend per Share}}{\text{Industry Normal Rate}} = \frac{2.50}{12.5\%} = \frac{2.50}{0.125} = ₹\ 20$

(c) Value of Equity/Business = No. of Shares × Value per Share

= 5 lakh × 20

= ₹ 100 lakhs

**Illustration 4.8:** Chandan Ltd. has declared dividend during the past five years as follows:

| Year | Rate of Dividend (%) |
|---|---|
| 2007-08 | 12 |
| 2008-09 | 15 |
| 2009-10 | 18 |
| 2010-11 | 21 |
| 2011-12 | 24 |

The average rate of return prevailing in the same industry is 15%. You are required to calculate the value per share of ₹ 10 of Chandan Ltd. and value of business assuming that company had issued 10 lakh shares.

**Solution:**

(a) Calculation of weighted average rate of dividend as the rate of dividend has been increasing every year, it is better to calculate weighted average rate of dividend.

| Year | Rate of Dividend (%) | Weight | Total Weight |
|---|---|---|---|
| 2007-08 | 12 | 1 | 12 |
| 2008-9 | 15 | 2 | 30 |
| 2009-10 | 18 | 3 | 54 |
| 2010-11 | 21 | 4 | 84 |
| 2011-12 | 24 | 5 | 120 |
| | | **15** | **300** |

$$\therefore \text{Weighted Average} = \frac{300}{15} = 20\%.$$

(b) $$\text{Value per Share} = \frac{\text{Company's Rate}}{\text{Industry Normal Rate}} \times \text{Nominal Value per Share}$$

$$= \frac{20}{15} \times 10 = ₹13.33.$$

(c) Value of Business = No. of Shares × Value per Share

= 10 lakh × 20

= ₹ 200 lakhs.

**Illustration 4.9:** Himalaya Drugs Ltd. has the capital base as follows:

(i) 10,00,000 Equity share of ₹ 10 each ₹ 5 per share paid-up, and

(ii) 25,000, 12% cumulative redeemable preference shares of ₹ 100 each fully paid-up.

The profit of the company for the year ended 31st March, 2012 were ₹ 60 lakhs. After setting apart amount for interest on borrowings, taxes and other provisions the net surplus available to the shareholders is estimated at ₹ 15 lakhs.

Enquiries in the stock market reveal that shares of companies engaged in similar business and declaring a dividend of 15% on equity shares are quoted at a premium of 20%. You are required to determine the value of equity share of the company as well as total equity valuations.

**Solution:**

(a) Calculation of Rate of Dividend

| | |
|---|---|
| Net surplus available | ₹ 15,00,000 |
| *Less*: Preference dividend | ₹ 3,00,000 |
| Amount available for equity shareholders | **12,00,000** |

$$\therefore \text{Co's Rate of Dividend} = \frac{\text{Amount of Dividend}}{\text{Equity Capital}} \times 100$$

$$= \frac{12{,}00{,}000}{50{,}00{,}000} \times 100 = 24\%.$$

(b) $$\text{Value per Equity Share} = \frac{\text{Rate of Dividend}}{\text{Industry Rate}} \times \text{Paid - up Value}$$

$$= \frac{24}{15} \times 5 = ₹\,8.$$

(c) Total Value of Equity = Value per Share × No. of Equity Share

= ₹ 8 × 10 lakhs

= ₹ 80 lakhs.

## (d) Return on Capital Employed

Return on Investment is a percentage of return on the total capital employed in the business. It provides an easily calculated and acceptable measure of economic performance of the business. It is calculated as follows:

$$\text{ROCE} = \frac{\text{Operating Profit}}{\text{Capital Employed}} \times 100$$

Operating profit is the profit before interest and taxes. The term interest means interest on borrowing. Interest on Government Securities or non-trading losses or expenses are to be excluded from the operating profit. The term Capital Employed is generally used in the following way:

Capital Employed = (Share Capital + Reserve and Surplus + Long-term Loans – Fictitious and Non-business Assets).

Return on capital employed is the end result of two forces, i.e., profit and capital. It measures how effectively the resources are put to use. Return on investment is an important means of measuring management success in profitably investing in company's assets. It is very much used in investment decision making.

ROCE is a single method which is required from the company whose shares or business are to be valued. It is based on the predetermined notion of the rate of return investor would expect on investment. The first step in the process of valuation is to select the past period of investigation. Then estimate the future maintainable profit after making any necessary adjustments. Then establish the acceptable market rate of return on capital invested in a similar type of company, allowing for the industry effect, the size of the company and the level of capital gearing. The next step is to capitalise maintainable profits at a rate established as the acceptable rate of return. The value of business is determined using the formula as under.

$$\text{Value of Business} = \frac{\text{Company's estimated future maintainable profit}}{\text{Industry's normal rate of return on capital employed}}$$

The limitation of this approach is that the estimates of earnings is usually based on historical earnings. The estimated earnings may be taken at simple average or weighted average.

**Illustration 4.10:** The net profit after tax of Uttam Steels Ltd. for the year ended 31st March, 2012 was ₹ 25 lakhs. The company expects to earn an average after tax profit of ₹ 30 lakhs in the next five years. The companies in similar business are yielding a post-tax accounting rate of return on capital employed is 20%. The company employs capital as 60% equity and 40% debt. You are required to calculate the value of business and value per share of the company assuming that the company had issued 5 lakh equity shares.

**Solution:**

(a) Company's future maintainable profit = ₹ 30 lakhs.

(b) $$\text{Value of Business} = \frac{\text{Future Maintainable Profit}}{\text{Return on Capital Employed}}$$

$$= \frac{₹\ 30 \text{ lakhs}}{20\%} = ₹\ 150 \text{ lakhs.}$$

(c) Value of Equity = 60% of 150 lakhs

= ₹ 90 lakhs.

(d) $$\text{Value per Share} = \frac{90}{5} = ₹\ 18.$$

**Illustration 4.11:** The profit after tax of Prime Industries Ltd. for the year ended 31st March, 2012 was ₹ 120 lakhs. The company is expecting to earn after tax profit of ₹ 150 lakhs in the next five years, All the companies in the similar business are earning a post-tax rate of return on capital employed at 25%. Calculate the value of business of the company based on rate of return on capital employed.

**Solution:**

(a) Company's expected future maintainable profit = ₹ 150 lakhs.

(b) Industry's normal rate of return on capital employed = 25%.

(c) $$\text{Value of Business} = \frac{\text{Estimated Future Maintainable Profit}}{\text{Normal Rate of Return}}$$

$$= \frac{150}{25} = ₹\ 600 \text{ lakhs.}$$

**Illustration 4.12:** From the following data available from the books of Twinkle Ltd. Calculate the value of business assuming that the company has issued 20 lakh equity shares of ₹ 10 each fully paid-up.

| Year 31st March | Capital Employed (₹ lakhs) | Profit (₹ lakhs) |
|---|---|---|
| 2008 | 200 | 30 |
| 2009 | 260 | 50 |
| 2010 | 330 | 60 |
| 2011 | 350 | 80 |
| 2012 | 410 | 110 |

The market expected rate of return on capital employed is 16 per cent.

**Solution:**

(a) Calculation of rate of return on capital employed.

As the profits have been increasing year after year, it is better to calculate weighted average

| Year 31st March | Capital Employed (₹ lakhs) | Profit (₹ lakhs) | ROCE (%) | Weight | Total |
|---|---|---|---|---|---|
| 2008 | 200 | 30 | 15 | 1 | 15.0 |
| 2009 | 260 | 50 | 19.2 | 2 | 38.4 |
| 2010 | 330 | 60 | 18.2 | 3 | 54.6 |
| 2011 | 350 | 80 | 22.9 | 4 | 91.6 |
| 2012 | 410 | 110 | 26.8 | 5 | 134.0 |
| Total | | | | **15** | **333.6** |

Company's Weighted Average Rate of Return on Capital Employed $= \frac{333.6}{15} = 22.24\%$.

(b) Market expected rate of return on capital employed = 16%.

(c) $\text{Value of Share} = \frac{\text{Company's Expected Rate of Return}}{\text{Market Expected Rate of Return}} \times \text{Nominal Value per Share}$

$$= \frac{22.24\%}{16\%} \times 10 = ₹13.90$$

(d) Value of Business = Value per Share × No of Equity Share

= ₹ 13.90 × 20 lakhs

= ₹ 278 lakhs

## 4.3 PEG RATIOS

Price Earnings to Growth ratio is the relation between P/E Ratio and Growth in EPS. It is determined as follows:

$$\text{PEG} = \frac{\text{P/E Ratio}}{\text{Growth in EPS}}$$

P/E Ratio is the relation between market price of a share and its earnings per share. It is expressed in number of times. Growth in earnings per share is the percentage increase in earnings per share over a period of times. For example, the EPS of a company in 2010 was ₹ 20 and it has increased to ₹ 25 in the year 2011. Thus, the growth in EPS is $\left(\frac{5}{20}\times 100\right) = 25\%$.

The value of PEG should be minimum then it is better or the performance of the company is better. This is one of the important factors which are considered for investment in the stock market or valuation of the companies/business.

**Illustration 4.13:** The data relating to India Cements are given for the two quarters as follows:

| Quarter | Stock Price ₹ | EPS Growth (%) | P/E Ratio |
|---|---|---|---|
| 30.9.2011 | 69.10 | 388.58 | 4.38 |
| 31.12.2011 | 100.80 | 426.84 | 15.85 |

You are required to determine PEG of both the quarter and comment on the performance of the share.

**Solution:**

(a) Calculation of PEG for Quarter ending 30.9.2011 $= \frac{\text{PE}}{\text{EPS Growth (\%)}}$

$$= \frac{11.22}{388.58\%} = 0.03 = 3\%$$

(b) Calculation of PEG for Quarter ending 31.12.2011 $= \frac{\text{PE}}{\text{EPS Growth (\%)}}$

$$= \frac{15.85}{426.84\%} = 0.04 = 4\%$$

PEG in the Quarter ending 30.9.2011 was 0.03 which was lower, hence the value of share was ₹ 69.10 but the PEG in the next quarter has increased and the value of share has also increased from ₹ 69.10 to ₹ 100.80 per share.

Thus, there is a relationship between value of share and growth in earnings per share.

**Illustration 4.14:** The following data are related to X Ltd. for the two years:

| | (₹ lakhs) | |
|---|---|---|
| **Year ended 31st March** | **2011** | **2012** |
| Equity share capital (₹ 10 each) | 50 | 50 |
| Secured loans at 15% | 25 | 20 |
| Unsecured loan @12.5% | 10 | 10 |
| Fixed assets | 30 | 30 |
| Investments | 5 | 5 |
| Operating profit | 25 | 30 |
| Income tax rate 30% | | |
| PEG | 0.40 | 0.50 |

You are required to find out the value of equity and value per share at X Ltd. as on 31.03.2012.

**Solution:**

(a) Calculation of EPS

| | (₹ lakhs) | |
|---|---|---|
| | **2011** | **2012** |
| Operating profit | 25 | 30 |
| – Interest | | |
| Secured loan | 3.75 | 3.00 |
| Unsecured loan | 1.25 | 1.25 |
| Profit before tax | 20 | 25.750 |
| *Less*: Tax | 6 | 7.725 |
| Profit after tax | 14 | 18.025 |
| No. of Eq. shares in lakhs | 5 | 5 |
| Earning per share | 2.8 | 3.60 |
| Growth in EPS | – | 28.57 |

(b) Calculation of P/E Ratio

$$\text{PEG} = \frac{\text{P/E Ratio}}{\text{Growth in EPS}}$$

$$\therefore \text{PE Ratio} = \text{PEG} \times \text{Growth in EPS}$$
$$= 0.5 \times 28.57$$
$$= 14.28 \text{ Times}$$

(c) $\therefore$ Market Price of share = P/E Ratio × EPS

$$= 14.28 \times 3.60$$
$$= ₹\ 51.41$$

(d) Value of Equity = No. of shares × Market price per share

$$= 5 \times 51.41$$
$$= ₹\ 257.05 \text{ lakhs.}$$

## 4.4 EV/EBIT MULTIPLES

The fundamental approach to valuation of business assets is the importance of company's fundamentals for its valuation. These methods ascertain the company's value on the basis of financial information that is relevant to company and its future. This type of valuation is also called as 'stand-alone'. valuation. An EBIT multiple expresses the company's value in relation to cash flow as ascertained from the income statement. EBIT can be easily taken from the audited financial statements and it is more stable over time. The use of cash flow in ascertaining of enterprise value is more appropriate because the cash flow generation capacity will determine the enterprise value (EV). The following formula is used to find out the value of an enterprise.

$$\frac{\text{EV}}{\text{EBIDT}} = \frac{\text{ROCE} - g}{\text{ROCE}\,(K_o - g)} \times (1 - t)(1 - d)$$

where

EV = Enterprise value

EBIDT = Earning before interest, depreciation and tax

ROCE = Return on capital employed
$K_o$ = Cost of capital
g = Growth rate
d = Depreciation as a % of EBIDT
t = Tax rate

Operating free cash flow is also considered in valuation of an enterprise. The operating free cash flow represents EBIDT as reduced by annual capital expenditure and extraordinary items, which can be ascertained from the published financial statements. The Enterprise Value is determined by using the following formula:

$$\frac{EV}{OPFCF} = \frac{ROCE - g}{ROCE \times (k - g)} \times (1 - t)$$

where

OPFCF is EBIDT – Estimated annual reinvestment – Inflation on working capital
ROCE – OPFCF/Capital stock

Operating multiples express the value of an enterprise in relation to a specific operational activity. This method considers the revenue generating unit specific to particular industry. The following formula is used to determine the Enterprise Value.

$$\frac{EV}{Unit} = \frac{ROCE - g}{ROCE\,(K_o - g)} \times \frac{NOPAT}{Unit}$$

where

NOPAT is net operating profit after tax
Unit = Unit of capacity or revenue generating unit

The revenue generating units after from industry to industry as follows:

| Industry | Multiple |
|---|---|
| Cement | EV/Metric Tonnes of Production |
| Automobile | EV/Number of Cars Produced |
| Power | EV/Kwh Production |
| Hotel | EV/Number of Rooms in the Hotel |

**Illustration 4.15:** A company has current operating income of ₹ 4,00,000 (EBIT). It has ₹ 10 lakhs of 10% debt outstanding. Its cost of equity capital is estimated to be 15 per cent. Determine the current value of the firm using EBIT approach.

**Solution:** Valuation of firm

| | |
|---|---|
| EBIT | ₹ 4,00,000 |
| *Less*: Interest | 1,00,000 |
| Earnings for equity holders | **3,00,000** |
| Equity capitalisation rate (Ke) | 0.15 |
| ∴ Market value of equity | ₹ 20,00,000 |
| Market value of debt | ₹ 10,00,000 |
| Market value of firm | **30,00,000** |

**Illustration 4.16:** The Evergreen Ltd. has to raise ₹ 50 lakh by issue of additional equity shares of ₹ 50 per share. The current capital structure of the company consists of 10 lakh equity shares. The tax rate is 35%, The company can also raise this amount by the sale of 10% debentures. You are required to:

(a) Calculate at what level of EBIT would EPS be the same whether new funds are raised by Debt or Equity.

(b) Determine the level of EBIT at which uncommitted earnings per share would be the same if sinking fund obligations amount to ₹ 5 lakhs per year.

**Solution:**

(a) Determination of Indifference Point

$$\text{Debt Alternative} = \frac{(x - i)(1 - t)}{N_1} = \frac{(x - 5\text{ lakhs})(1 - .35)}{10\text{ lakhs}}$$

$$\text{Equity Alternative} = \frac{x(1 - t)}{N_2} = \frac{x(1 - 0.35)}{11\text{ lakhs}}$$

$$\therefore \frac{(x - 5,00,000)(0.65)}{10,00,000} = \frac{x(0.65)}{11,00,000}$$

$$\therefore x = ₹\ 55,00,000$$

| **Particulars** | **10% Debt (₹)** | **Equity (₹)** |
|---|---|---|
| EBIT | 55,00,000 | 55,00,000 |
| *Less*: Interest | 5,00,000 | – |
| EBT | **50,00,000** | **55,00,000** |
| *Less*: Taxes | 17,50,000 | 19,25,000 |
| PAT | 32,50,000 | 35,75,000 |
| No. of equity shares | 10,00,000 | 11,00,000 |
| ∴ EPS | ₹ 3.25 | ₹ 3.25 |

(b) Determination of Indifference Point with Sinking Fund

$$\text{Debt Alternative} = \frac{(x - i)(1 - t) - s}{N_1} \qquad \text{Equity Alternative} = \frac{x(1 - t)}{N_2}$$

$$= \frac{(x - 5,00,000)(0.65) - 5,00,000}{10,00,000} = \frac{0.65x}{11,00,000}$$

$$\therefore x = ₹\ 1,39,61,538$$

## 4.5 PRICE/BOOK VALUE MULTIPLE

The book value multiple reflects the market value of equity shares in relation to the company's book value. The book value of an asset refers to the amount of which an asset is shown in the balance sheet of a firm. It is the sum equal to the initial acquisition cost of an asset less accumulated depreciation. Book value of a business is the total book value of all valuable assets less external liabilities. Fictitious assets like deferred revenue expenditure, preliminary expenses and accumulated loss. It is also referred to as net worth of the business. Book value is, thus, the adjusted book value of total assets less adjusted book value of liabilities. This ratio is called as price/book value or P/BV Ratio.

This is the simplest approach to valuing the firm. It is based on the information found in the balance sheet of a firm. However, the accuracy of the book value approach depends on how well the net book values of the assets reflect their fair market values. Therefore, in most real life situations, the book value approach has limited applicability. The value of an equity share is determined as follows:

$$\text{Value per Share} = \text{Book Value per Share} \times \text{P/BV Ratio.}$$

Price/Book Value Ratio is determined as follows:

$$\text{P/BV Ratio} = \frac{\text{Market Value per Share}}{\text{Book Value per Share}}$$

The value of Equity is determined by multiplying the market price per share and no. of equity shares issued by the company.

**Illustration 4.7:** The balance sheets of Heera Ltd. as on 31st March, 2012 was as follows:

| Liabilities | ₹ lakhs | Assets | | ₹ lakhs |
|---|---|---|---|---|
| Equity share capital (₹ 10 each) | 15 | Fixed Assets | | 33 |
| | | Investments | | 2 |
| Reserve and Surplus | 11 | **Current Asset** | | |
| Secured loan | 14 | Cash Bank | 2 | |
| Unsecured loan | 7 | Debtors | 12 | |
| Current liabilities | 13 | Stock | 10 | 24 |
| | | Preliminary Exp. | | 01 |
| Total | **60** | Total | | **60** |

The equity shares are traded in the stock market at ₹ 50 each. Determine the Price/Book Value Ratio.

**Solution:**

(a) Calculation of net Assets

| | | ₹ lakhs |
|---|---|---|
| Fixed Assets | | 33 |
| Current Assets | | 24 |
| Total | | 57 |
| *Less*: **Outside Liabilities** | | |
| Secured loan | 14 | |
| Unsecured loan | 07 | |
| Current liabilities | 13 | 34 |
| Net worth | | 23 |

$$\text{Book Value per Share} = \frac{\text{Net Assets}}{\text{No. of Eq. Shares}}$$

$$= \frac{23}{1.5} = ₹\,15.33$$

$$\therefore \text{Price Book Value Ratio} = \frac{\text{Market Price}}{\text{Book Value per Share}}$$

$$= \frac{50}{15.33} = 3.3 \text{ Times}$$

**Illustration 4.18:** The following is the Balance sheet of A Ltd. as on 31.3.2012:

| Liabilities | ₹ lakhs | Assets | | ₹ lakhs |
|---|---|---|---|---|
| Preference share capital (₹ 100 each) | 450 | Fixed Assets | | 400 |
| Equity share capital (₹ 10 each) | 100 | Investments | | 120 |
| | | **Current Asset** | | |
| Preserve and Surplus | 150 | Stock | 200 | |
| Bank loan | 200 | Debtors | 200 | |
| Current Liabilities | 100 | Cash bank | 80 | 480 |
| | **1,000** | | | **1,000** |

The P/BV ratio of the industry is 4.5 times. Determine the value of firm.

**Solution:**

(a) Calculation of book value per share

| | | |
|---|---|---|
| Fixed Assets | | ₹ 400 lakhs |
| Current Assets | | ₹ 480 lakhs |
| Total | | 880 |
| *Less*: (1) Bank loan | 200 | |
| (2) Current Liabilities | 100 | 300 |
| Net Assets | | 580 |
| *Less*: Preference share capital | | 450 |
| Balance to equityholders | | **130** |

$$\text{Book Value per Share} = \frac{130}{10} = ₹\,13$$

(b) Calculation of market price per share

$$\text{P/BV Ratio} = \frac{\text{Market Price per Share}}{\text{Book Value per Share}}$$

$$4.5 \text{ Times} = \frac{\text{M. P.}}{13}$$

$\therefore$ Market Price per Share = $13 \times 4.5$

= ₹ 58.50

(c) Value of firm (Equity) = M.P. per Share × No. of Equity Shares

= $58.50 \times 10$

= ₹ 585 lakhs.

## 4.6 SALES MULTIPLES

Sales multiple reflects the value of enterprise in relation to its revenues. Revenue multiples are used to calculate both enterprise value and value of equity. Revenue multiples are generally used for valuation of firms which are not currently profitable. The fundamental multiple based on sales or revenues can be expressed as follows:

$$\frac{EV}{Sales} = \frac{ROCE - g}{(ROCE)\,(K_o - g)} \times (1 - t)M.$$

where

ROCE = Return on capital employed

$K_o$ = Cost of capitalization

g = Growth rate

t = Tax rate

M = EBIDT Margin in per cent.

**Illustration 4.19:** The following financial information is available for Delta Ltd.

| PBDIT | ₹ 18 lakhs |
|---|---|
| Book value of assets | ₹ 90 lakhs |
| Sales | ₹ 125 lakhs |

Based on an evaluation of several companies X, Y and Z have been found to be comparable to Delta Ltd. The financial information of these companies is given below:

| Particular | X | Y | Z |
|---|---|---|---|
| PBDIT (₹ lakhs) | 12 | 15 | 20 |
| Book value of assets (₹ lakhs) | 75 | 80 | 100 |
| Sales (₹ lakhs) | 80 | 100 | 160 |
| Market value (₹ lakhs) | 150 | 240 | 360 |
| MV/PBDIT | 12.5 | 16 | 18 |
| MV/BV | 2 | 3 | 3.6 |
| MV/Sales | 1.9 | 2.4 | 2.3 |

Taking into account the characteristics of Delta Ltd. and X, Y and Z, the following multiples appear responsible for Delta Ltd.

MV/PBDIT = 17

MV/Book value = 3

MV/Sales = 2.2

Determine the value of Delta Ltd.

**Solution:**

(a) Calculation of market value Delta Ltd.

1. MV = 17 × PBDIT = 17 × 18 = ₹ 306 lakhs
2. MV = 3 × B.V. = 3 × 90 = ₹ 270 lakhs
3. MV = 2.2 × Sales = 2.2 × 125 = ₹ 275 lakhs

(b) Market value based on sales multiple is ₹ 270 lakhs. However, other values are different. Hence, it would be ideal to take average value as follows:

$$\text{M.V.} = \frac{306 + 270 + 275}{3} = \frac{851}{3} = ₹\ 283.7\ \text{lakhs}.$$

## 4.7 CHOOSING THE RIGHT MULTIPLE

The fundamental approach to valuations of business assets is the importance of companies fundamentals for valuation. These methods ascertain the company's value on the basis of financial information that is relevant to company and its future. The following multiples can be used for determination of the value of firm:

1. Sales Multiple
2. Operation Profit Multiple
3. Operating Free Cash Flow Multiple
4. Operating Multiple
5. Price/Earning Multiple
6. Price/Book Value Multiple

Choosing the right multiple depends upon the need and purpose of valuation. It also depends upon the information available with the company. Again the different multiple can be used in different times and needs. However, the Operating Free Cash Flow Multiple is the most scientific and suitable multiple for any valuation. However, it requires calculation of free cash flow.

## 4.8 EXERCISES

1. What is relative valuation of business?
2. What is Price/Earning Ratio? How is business valued under this approach?
3. What are the methods used in valuation of business based on company's fundamentals?
4. "No method of valuation of shares by itself is perfect: A combination of different relatives will give a proper valuation". Explain with examples.
5. Write short note on 'pricing multiples'.
6. "Earning shown by income statement need to be adjusted for valuation". Explain this statements.
7. Write short notes on the following:
   (a) Book Value Multiple (b) PEG Ratios
   (c) Relative Valuation (d) Sales Multiples
   (e) Earnings Yield Approach
8. Following is the Balance sheet of X Ltd. as on 31st March, 2012:

| Liabilities | ₹ lakhs | Assets | | ₹ lakhs |
|---|---|---|---|---|
| 11% Preference capital | 40 | Fixed assets | 150 | |
| Equity capital | 120 | Depreciation | 30 | 120 |
| Reserve and Surplus | 120 | Stock | 150 | |
| 10% Debentures | 100 | Debtors | 200 | |
| Creditors | 100 | Cash bank | 15 | 365 |
| Provision for tax | 10 | Preliminary expenses | | 5 |
| | **490** | | | **490** |

**Additional Information:**

1. If firm of professional valuers has provided the following market estimate of its various assets as follows:

   Fixed Assets ₹ 130 lakhs, Stock 155 lakhs, Debtors 145 lakhs. All other assets are to be taken at their balance sheet value.

2. The company is yet to declare and pay dividend on preference shares.

   You are required to compute the value of firm as per book value and market value bases.

9. Uttam Steels Ltd. has earned a profit at ₹ 240 lakhs after tax for the year ended 31st March, 2012, the company is expecting to earn an after tax profit of ₹ 300 lakhs in the next five years. All the companies in the similar business are yielding a post-tax accounting rate of return on capital employed at 24%. You are required to calculate the value of the company based on rate of return on capital employed.

   (Answer: ₹ 1,250 lakhs)

10. From the following data available from the books of Tata Timeken Ltd. Calculate the value of the company based on return on capital Employed:

| Year ended on 31st March | Capital Employed (₹ lakhs) | Profit (₹ lakhs) |
|---|---|---|
| 2012 | 410 | 110 |
| 2011 | 250 | 80 |
| 2010 | 330 | 60 |
| 2009 | 260 | 50 |
| 2008 | 200 | 30 |

The market expectation being 16%. The company has issued 10 lakh equity shares of ₹ 10 each.

(Answer: Value per share ₹ 13.90, Value of firm ₹ 139 lakhs)

11. Parag Ltd. is having an issued and subscribed capital of 5,00,000 equity shares of ₹ 10 each fully paid-up. The company's after tax profits for the year 2011 amounted to ₹ 28 lakhs. The average present stock exchange price of the company's share is ₹ 19. The P/E Ratio of four listed companies engaged in the similar business are as follows:

| Company | 2009 | 2010 | 2011 |
|---|---|---|---|
| A Ltd. | 5.7 | 6.3 | 7.1 |
| B Ltd. | 6.5 | 5.9 | 6.8 |
| C Ltd. | 7.4 | 6.8 | 7.0 |
| D Ltd. | 5.0 | 5.9 | 6.1 |

Calculate the value of business of Parag Ltd. based on P/E Ratio of the industry.

(Answer: ₹ 178.57 lakhs)

12. The capital structure of Q Ltd. is as follows:

| | |
|---|---|
| 12% Preference shares of ₹ 100 each | ₹ 5,00,000 |
| Equity share of ₹ 10 each | ₹ 80,00,000 |
| Reserve and Surplus | ₹ 4,00,000 |
| 10% Debentures | ₹ 6,00,000 |
| 12% Term loan | ₹ 7,00,000 |
| Total | **₹ 30,00,000** |

The average annual profit before payment of tax and interest is ₹ 6,00,000. The income tax rate is 30%. You are required to determine the value of equity shares of the company if the applicable P/E Ratio is 10.

(Answer: ₹ 32.40)

13. The following financial information is available for D Ltd.

| | |
|---|---|
| PBDIT | ₹ 180 lakhs |
| Book value of Assets | ₹ 900 lakhs |
| Sales | ₹ 1,250 lakhs |

The following multiplies are to be applied to the financial number of the company

| | |
|---|---|
| MV/PBDIT | 15 |
| MV/ Book value | 3 |
| MV/ Sales | 2.5 |

You are required to calculate the fair value of the firm.

(Answer: ₹ 2842 lakhs)

14. H Ltd. agrees to acquire 'S' Ltd. based on the capitalization of lost three years profits of 'S' Ltd. at an earnings yield of 16%. Profits of 'S' Ltd. for the last there years were ₹ 60 lakhs to ₹ 80 lakhs and ₹ 70 lakh respectively. Calculate the value of Business on the earnings yield Basis.

(Answer: ₹ 437.5 lakhs)

15. Akruti Ltd. has an issued and subscribed capital of ₹ 50,00,000 divided into ₹ 10 shares each. The company declared a dividend of ₹ 10 lakhs during the last five years and expects to maintain the same level in future. The control and ownership of the company is lying in few hands of director and their family members. The average dividend yield for listed companies in the same line of business is 10%. You are required to determine the value of business using the concept of dividend yield.

(Answer: ₹ 100 lakhs).

# Chapter 5 BRAND VALUATION


5.1 Introduction
5.2 Meaning of Brand
5.3 Top 10 Bands in the World
5.4 Category-wise Brands
5.5 Most Valued Brands
5.6 Contribution of Brands to Shareholder Value
5.7 Brand Valuation
5.8 Strategic Brand Management
5.9 Social Value of Brands
5.10 Exercises


## 5.1 INTRODUCTION

For the last quarter of the 20th century, tangible assets were regarded as the main source of business value. These tangible assets included land, building, manufacturing and financial assets. These assets were valued at cost or outstanding value as shown in the balance sheet. The market was aware of intangibles but their specific value remained unclear and was not specifically quantified. The evaluation of profitability and performance of business focuses on indication such as return on investment assets or equity that excluded intangibles from the denominator. Measures of price relatives also excluded the value of intangible assets as these are absent from accounting book values. Management failed to recognize the importance of intangibles at least in India. Brands, technology, patents and employees were always at the heart of corporate success, but rarely and explicitly valued, major brand owners like Coca-Cola, Proctor Gamble, Unilever and Nestle were aware of the importance of their brands, as indicated by their creation of brand managers. World's most valuable Brand, Coca-Cola is 118 years old company.

The increasing recognisition of the value of intangibles came with the continuous increase in the gap between companies' book values and their stock market valuations. Thus, today the majority of business value is derived from intangibles. Therefore, the management's attention to these assets has increased substantially.

## 5.2 MEANING OF BRANDS

"The brand is a special intangible that in many business it is the most important assets". This is due to the economic impact of the brand.

Brand, technology patents and employees are always at the heart of corporate success. However, they are rarely explicitly valued. Their value was assumed in the overall assets value.

World's most valuable brand, Coca-Cola is more than 120 years old. The majority of the world's most valuable brands have been around for more than 60 years. This is with an estimated average life span for a company of 25 years. Many brands have survived a string of different corporate owners. Brands influence the choices of customers, employees, investors and government authorities. Such influence is essential for commercials success and creation of shareholder value. Non-profit organizations and social organization have also started embracing the brand as they are assets for sponsorships, donations and volunteers.

## 5.3 TOP 10 BANDS IN THE WORLD

The top 10 Brands for the year ended 31st March are as follows:

**Top 10 Brands**

| Rank | For 2011 | For 2012 |
|---|---|---|
| 1 | Nokia | Nokia |
| 2 | Tata | Tata |
| 3 | Sony | LG |
| 4 | LG | Samsung |
| 5 | Samsung | Sony |
| 6 | Reliance | Maruti Suzuki |
| 7 | Maruti Suzuki | Bajaj |
| 8 | LIC | LIC |
| 9 | Airtel | Airtel |
| 10 | Titan | Reliance |

***Source***: *Business Standard* 17th January, 2012.

The Brands Trust Report published in the *Business Standard* on 17th January, 2012 has conducted research on 61 components of trust with 2,718 companies from 15 cities. Among the Automobiles, Maruti Suzuki featured in the list of top 10 Brands. In the financial services LIC appeared in the top 10 but SBI, ICICI Bank, HDFC have been rated as the most trusted. Nokia and Tata Brands have captured 1st and 2nd place in both the years. Thus many Indian companies have performed better with their brands. Category-wise toppers in the list of most trusted brands are as follows:

| Sr. No. | Category | Brand |
|---|---|---|
| 1 | Apparels-Fabric | Raymond |
| 2 | Construction | DLF |
| 3 | Footwear | Bata |
| 4 | Retail Multi Brand Outlet | Big Bazaar |
| 5 | Soft Drink | Pepsi |
| 6 | Health Care | Dabur |
| 7 | Tea | Tata Tea |
| 8 | Domestic Airlines | Air India |
| 9 | Sport Accessories | Reebok |
| 10 | Beauty | Ponds |

The above list indicates that many Indian companies have developed their brands during last two decades.

## 5.4 CATEGORY-WISE BRANDS

India's most trusted brands are given below:

| Category | Most Trusted Brand |
|---|---|
| Tea | Tata Tea |
| Alcoholic Beverages | Kingfisher |
| Car | Maruti Suzuki Dzire |
| Insurance | Life Insurance Corporation |
| Beauty | Ponds |
| Apparels | Raymond |
| Construction | DLF |
| Appliances | LG |
| Watches | Titan |
| Paints | Asian Paint |
| Footwear | Bata |
| Health Care | Dabur |
| Domestic Airline | Air India |
| Retail Multi Brand Outlet | Big Bazaar |
| Electronics | Sony |

***Source:*** Brand Trust Report published in *Business Standard* 17th January, 2012.

Brand Trust Report is based on primary research conducted in 61 components of trust a proprietary tool of Trust Research Advisory. The research was conducted with 2,718 influence respondents from 15 cities generating more than two million data-points from 1,200 hour research. Nokia and Tata have retained their first and second positions in the report which lists India's 1,000 most trusted brands.

## 5.5 MOST VALUED BRANDS

Most valued brands in India as well as global are as follows:

**Most Valued Brands**

| Indian | | | Global | | |
|---|---|---|---|---|---|
| **Sr. No.** | **Brand** | **Value ($ billion)** | **Sr. No.** | **Brand** | **Value ($ billion)** |
| 1 | Tata | 16.34 | 1 | Apple | 70.60 |
| 2 | Airtel | 5.22 | 2 | Google | 47.46 |
| 3 | SBI | 4.68 | 3 | Microsoft | 45.81 |
| 4 | Reliance | 4.36 | 4 | IBM | 39.13 |
| 5 | IOL | 3.66 | 5 | Walmart | 38.31 |

***Source*: Brand Finance, *Business Standard* 20.3.2012.**

In India's Tata's is the most valuable brand having value of $16.34 billion. Other brands are having more or less same value. SBI is the banking brand in the public sector. Among the Global brands computer software companies are at the top having brand value 45 to 70 billion dollar. IBM is the old brand and Walmart is the brand in the retail sector.

## 5.6 CONTRIBUTION OF BRANDS TO SHAREHOLDER VALUE

The brands have contributed towards the shareholder value creation. The value of brand and its contribution to market capitalization of parent company are given below:

**Contribution of Brands to Shareholder Value**

| Sr. No. | Company | Brand Value (2002) ($ billion) | Brand Contribution to Market Capitalization of Parent Company (%) |
|---|---|---|---|
| 1 | Coca-Cola | 69.6 | 51 |
| 2 | Microsoft | 64.1 | 21 |
| 3 | IBM | 51.2 | 39 |
| 4 | G.E. | 41.3 | 14 |
| 5 | Intel | 30.9 | 22 |
| 6 | Nokia | 30.0 | 51 |
| 7 | Disney | 29.3 | 68 |
| 8. | McDonald's | 26.4 | 71 |
| 9 | Marlboro | 24.2 | 20 |
| 10 | Mercedez Benz | 21.0 | 47 |

***Source*: Business Week, Interbrand J.P. Morgan League Table, 2002.**

Studies by academics from Harvard and University of South Colombia and by Interbrand of the companies featured in the Best Global Brands League Table indicates that companies with strong brands outperformed the market in respect of several indices. Today, leading companies focus their management efforts on intangible assets. The economic contribution made by the brands to companies is considerable. A study by Interbrand in association with J.P. Morgan pointed out that an average brand accounts for more than one-third of shareholder value. The Coca-Cola brand alone accounts for 51 per cent of the stock market value of the company. This is despite the fact that the company owns a large portfolio of other drink's brands such as Sprite and Fanta.

## 5.7 BRAND VALUATION

Leading companies focus their management efforts on intangible assets such as brands. Forel motor company reduced its physical asset base in favor of investing in intangibles. It has spent about $12 billion to acquire prestigious brand such as Jaguar, Aston Martin, Volvo and Land Rover. Samsung has been spending about 7.5 per cent of its annual revenues on Research and Development. Thus, it is about brands and brand building and consumer relationship. The wave of brand acquisition started in late 1980s. Accounting practice for so-called goodwill did not deal with the increasing importance of intangible assets. In UK, France, Australia it was possible to recognize the value of acquired brands as identifiable intangible assets and to put these on the balance sheet of the acquiring company. The recognition of brands, as intangible assets made use of grey area of accounting, whereby companies were not encouraged to include brands in the balance sheet but nor were they prevented from doing so. By the late 1980s, the recognition of the value of acquired brands on the balance sheet prompted a similar recognition of internally generated brands as valuable financial assets within a company. In 1988, Rank Hovis McDougal a leading UK conglomerate played heavily on the power of its brands to successfully defend a hostile takeover bid by Goodman Relder Wattie. The company's defence strategy was involved carrying out an exercise that demonstrated the value of Goodman's brand portfolio. It was the first independent brand valuation establishing that it was possible to value brands not only when they had been acquired, but also when they had been created by the company itself. Both the companies included in their financial account the value of both the internally generated and acquired brands under intangible assets on the balance sheets. Today, many companies have recognised acquired brands on their balance sheets. Some companies have been using the balance sheet recognition of their brands as an investor-relations tool by providing historic brand values and using brand value as a financial performance indicator.

UK, Australia and New Zealand have been leading the way by allowing acquired brands to appear on the balance sheet and providing detailed guidelines on how to deal with acquired brands. The UK Accounting Standards Board introduced FRS 10 and 11 on the treatment of goodwill on the balance sheet. The International Accounting Standards Board followed this standard with 38. Most international companies who wish to raise funds in the US capital markets were required to adhere to US GAAP. The principal stipulation of all these accounting standards are that acquired goodwill needs to be capitalized on the Balance sheet and amortized accounting to its useful life. However, brands can claim infinite life and do not have to be subjected to amortization. The companies have to perform annual impairment tests. If the value is the same or higher than the initial valuation, the value of assets on the balance sheet remains the same. The assets need to be written down to the lower value if the impairment value is lower. The valuation needs to be performed on the business unit that generates the revenues and profit. The Discounted Cash Flow Method and Market Value Approaches are the recommended methods of brand valuation.

## 5.7.1 Need for Brand Valuation

Companies find brand valuation helpful for the following:

1. To make decision on business investment.
2. To measure the return on brand investments.
3. To allocate marketing expenditure according to the benefit of cash business unit derives from the brand assets.
4. To organize and optimize the use of different brands in the business.
5. To manage a portfolio of brands across a variety of markets.
6. To assess fair transfer prices for the use of brands in subsidiary companies.
7. To determine brand royalty rates for optimal exploitation of the brand asset through licensing the brand to third parties.
8. To capitalize brand assets on the balance sheet according to US GAAP.
9. Brand Valuation is used for both the initial valuation and the periodical impairment tests for the derived values.
10. To know how much brands have contributed towards shareholder value creation.

## 5.7.2 Approaches to Brand Valuation

The brand valuation approaches were established in 1980 that could fairly claim to understand and assess the specific value of brands. The idea of putting a separate value on brands has how been widely accepted. Today a number of brand valuation models have been developed. The major brand valuation approaches are as follows:

### (a) Research-based Approach

There are brand equity models that use consumer research to assess the relative performance of brands. These model measure consumer behaviour and attitudes that have an impact on the economic performance on brands. These models try to explain, interpret and measure consumer's perceptions that influence purchase behaviour. These include a wide range of perceptive measures such as levels of awareness, knowledge, familiarity, relevance, specific image attributes, purchase consideration preferences, satisfaction and recommendations. Some of these models also add behavioural measure such as market share and relative prices.

The various measures are arranged either in hierarchic order to provide handles that lead from awareness to preference and purchase, relative to their impact on overall consumer perception to provide an overall brand equity score or measure. A change in one or a combination of indicator is expected to influence consumer's purchasing behaviour which may affect the financial value of the brand.

### (b) Financially-driven Approaches

A brand should provide a clear link between the specific marketing indicators and the financial performance. A brand can perform strongly according to consumer-based research but still fail to create financial and shareholder value. Thus understanding, interpretation and measurement of brand equity indicators are crucial for assessing the financial value of brands. They are the key measure of consumer's purchasing behaviour upon which the success of the brand depends. The financially-driven approaches are as follows:

(i) **Cost-based approach:** Cost-based approach defines the value of a brand as the aggregation of all historic costs incurred or replacement costs required in bringing the brand to its current state of affairs. It includes development costs, marketing costs, Advertising and Communication costs.

(ii) **Comparables:** Comparable can provide an interesting cross-check even though they may never be relied on solely for valuing brands. This approach is to arrive at a value for a brand on the basis of some companies. However, the value creation of brands in the same category can be very different even through most of the other aspects of the underlying business are similar or identical.

(iii) **Premium price:** The primary purpose of brands is not necessarily to obtain a price premium but rather to secure the highest level of future demand. The value generation of the brands lies in securing future volume rather than securing a premium. It is true for many durable as well as non-durable consumer goods. The value of brand is calculated as the net present value of future price premiums that a branded product can command over an unbranded product.

(iv) **Economic use:** This approach is exclusively driven by brand equity measures and financial measures. It is the most widely recognized and accepted valuation method for brand valuation. It has been used in more than 3,500 brand valuation worldwide. The economic use approach is based on fundamental marketing and financial principles. The marketing principle relates to the commercial functions that brands perform within business. Brands help to generate customer demand and customer demand translates into revenues. The financial principle relates to the net present value of future expected earnings. Brand's future earnings are identified and then discounted to a net present value using a discount rate that reflects the risk of those earnings being realized.

### 5.7.3 Steps in Valuation of Brands

The following are the steps in valuation of brand of a company:

**(a) Market Segmentation**

Brands influence customer choice and the influence varies depending on the market in which the brand operates. Therefore, there is a need for splitting the brand's markets into homogeneous groups of customers according to applicable criteria. The criteria may be product, service, distribution channel, consumption patterns, geography, existing and new customers. The brand is valued in each segment and the sum of the segment valuations is the total value of brands.

**(b) Financial Analysis**

Analysis of the forecast revenues and earnings from intangibles generated by the brand for each of the distinct segments are made as per make segmentation. Intangible earnings are brand revenues less operating costs applicable taxes and a change for the capital employed.

**(c) Demand Analysis**

Analysis of the demand for products and service in the markets in which operates has to be made in order to determine the proportion of intangible earnings are attributable to the demand. It is measured by an indicator known as role of branding index. This is done by identifying the various drivers of demand for the branded business. Then the degree to which cash driver is directly influenced by the brand is determined. The role of branding index represents the percentage of intangible earnings that are generated by the brand. Brand earnings are calculated by multiplying the role of branding index by intangible earnings.

### (d) Competitive Benchmarking

They determine the competitive strengths and weaknesses of the brand to derive the specific brand discount rate that reflects the risk profile of its expected future earnings. This comprises extensive competitive benchmarking and a structured evaluation of the brand's market, stability, leadership position, growth trends, support, geographic foot print and legal protection.

### (e) Brand Value Calculation

Brand value is the net present value of the forecast brand earnings, discounted by the brand discount rate. The net present value calculation comprises both the forecast period and the period beyond, reflecting the ability of brands to continue generating future earnings.

**Illustration 5.1:** The following data is related to Delta Ltd a company having a share in branded portion as well as in unbranded portion.

| | |
|---|---|
| Branded revenue | ₹ 500 per unit |
| Unbranded revenue | ₹ 120 per unit |
| Branded cost | ₹ 350 per unit |
| Unbranded cost | ₹ 100 per unit |
| Research & Development cost | ₹ 20 lakhs |
| Branded products | 1 lakh units |
| Unbranded products | 40,000 units |
| Tax rate | 30% |
| Capitalization factor | 18% |

You are required to calculate the brand value of the company.

**Solution:**

(i) The net revenue from the branded products = Revenue – Costs

= [1,00,000 × 500 – 1,00,000 × 350]

= ₹ 500 lakhs – 350 lakhs

= ₹ 150 lakhs.

(ii) Net Revenue from unbranded products = Revenue – Costs

= 40,000 (120 – 100)

= ₹ 8,00,000

(iii) Profit after tax (for branded products)

| | **₹ lakhs** |
|---|---|
| Profit from branded product | 150 lakhs |
| – Profit from unbranded product | 8 lakhs |
| – R & D Expenditure | 20 lakhs |
| Net profit | 122 lakhs |

PAT = 122 (1 – 0.3)

= ₹ 85.4 lakhs.

(iv) $\text{Brand Value} = \dfrac{\text{PAT}}{\text{Capitalization Rate}}$

$= \dfrac{₹\,85.4\text{ lakhs}}{18\%}$

$= ₹\,474.44\text{ lakhs}$

**Illustration 5.2:** The following is the financial data of Infosys Ltd, an IT Company.

| Particular | ₹ lakhs | | |
|---|---|---|---|
| | **31.3.10** | **31.3.11** | **31.3.12** |
| Earnings before Int. & Tax | 150 | 320 | 700 |
| Non-branded income | 5 | 30 | 50 |
| Inflation compound factor @80% | 1.18 | 1.09 | 1.00 |
| Charges of capital (% of average capital employed) | 5 | 5 | 5 |
| Average capital employed | | | 1,100 |
| Income tax rate | | | 30% |
| Capitalization factor | | | 16% |

You are required to calculate the Brand Value of Infosys Ltd.

**Solution:**

**Infosys Ltd.**

**Computation of Brand Value**

| Particulars | (₹ cr) | | |
|---|---|---|---|
| | **2010** | **2011** | **2012** |
| EBIT | 150 | 320 | 700 |
| – Non-branded value | 5 | 30 | 50 |
| Adjusted profits | 145 | 290 | 650 |
| Inflation compound factor @8% | 1.18 | 1.09 | 1.00 |
| Present value of profit | 171.1 | 316 | 650 |
| Weightage factor | 1 | 2 | 3 |
| Weighted profit | 171.1 | 632 | 1,896 |
| Average profit | | | 450 |
| Capital charge | | | 55 |
| Brand related | | | 395 |
| Income Tax @30% | | | 118.5 |
| Brand earnings | | | 276.5 |
| Capitalization factor | | | 16% |

$$\text{Brand Value} = \frac{276.5}{16\%} = ₹\,1{,}728.12\text{ cores}$$

## 5.8 STRATEGIC BRAND MANAGEMENT

Brand Valuation helps the companies to establish value-based systems for brand management. Recognition of the economic value of brand has increased the demand for effective brand management. Economic value creation becomes the focus of brand management. Companies have used brand valuation to help them refocus their business on their brands and to create an economic rationale for branding decisions. Many companies have made brand value creation as part of remuneration criteria for senior marketing executives. The companies are keen to establish procedures for the management of brands that are aligned with those for other business assets, as well as the company. Many companies have adopted brand valuation as a brand management tool.

Brand Valuation is useful for the companies in the following ways:

(i) To make decision on business investments.

(ii) To measure the return on brand investments based on brand's value and to arrive at Return on Investment, which can be directly compared with other investments.

(iii) To make decision on brand investments.

(iv) To make decision on licensing the brand to subsidiary companies.

(v) To turn the marketing department from a cost center into a profit center by connecting brand investments and brand returns.

(vi) To allocate marketing expenditure according to the benefit each business unit derives from the brand asset.

(vii) To organize the use of different brands in the business according to their respective economic value contribution.

(viii) To decide the appropriate branding after merger according to a clear economic rationale.

(ix) To manage a portfolio of brands across a variety of markets, inside as well as outside the country.

Financial transaction where brand valuation helps in a variety of brand-related transaction with external parties are given below:

(i) To assess fair transfer prices for the use of brands in subsidiary companies.

(ii) To determine brand royalty rates for optimal exploitation of the brand asset through licensing the brand to third party.

(iii) To capitalize brand asset on the balance sheet according to specific standards of the country.

(iv) To determine the price of brand assets in mergers and acquisitions.

(v) To determine the contribution of brand to joint ventures to establish profit sharing investment requirements and shareholding in the venture.

(vi) To use brand for securitization of debt facilities in which the right for the economic exploitations of brands are used as collateral.

## 5.9 SOCIAL VALUE OF BRAND

Brands also create substantial social as well as economic value as a result of increased competition, improved product performance and pressure on brand owner to behave in socially responsible ways. The economic value of brands is now widely accepted, but their social value is not yet widely accepted in the society. The ambiguity of global mega-brands has made branding the focus of discount for money forces around the world. There is a link between brands and exploitation of wastes in developing countries like India and the homogenization of culture-brands are accused of stifling competion and tarnishing the virtues of the capitalist system by encouraging monopoly and limiting consumer choices.

Competition fosters product development and improvement. It is based on performance as well as price which is the nature of brand competition. A study in Europe revealed that the less-branded businesses launch few products and invest significantly less in the development. They have a few product advantages than their branded counterparts. The need to keep brands relevant promotes increased investments in Research and Development which leads to a continuous process of product improvement and development. Brand creators are accountable for both the quality and the performance of their branded products and services and for their ethical practices. A number of high profile brands have been accused of unethical practices. The honest companies are admitting the gap they have to bridge in terms of ethical behaviour.

## 5.10 EXERCISES

1. What is a brand? What are the advantages of brand?
2. What is brand valuation? What are the step in valuation of brand?
3. How is the brand valuations useful to the companies?
4. What are the approaches to valuation of brand?
5. The following data relates to Dempo Ltd.

| | (₹ lakhs) | | |
|---|---|---|---|
| **Particular** | **2010** | **2009** | **2008** |
| EBIT | 696 | 326 | 156 |
| Non-branded income | 53 | 35 | 04 |
| Inflation compound factor | 1.00 | 1.087 | 1.181 |
| Charge of capital @8% | 5% | | |
| Average capital employed | 1,112 | | |
| Income tax rate | 35% | | |
| Capitalization factor | 16% | | |

You are required to calculate the brand value for Dempo Ltd.

(Answer: ₹ 1.630 lakhs)

6. The following data is related to a company having a share in branded portion as well as non-branded portion.

| Branded revenue | ₹ 1,000 per unit |
|---|---|
| Unbranded revenue | 240 per unit |
| Branded cost | 700 per unit |
| Unbranded cost | 200 per unit |
| Research & Development cost | ₹ 40 lakhs |
| Branded products | 2 lakhs units |
| Unbranded product | 80,000 units |
| Income tax rate | 30% |
| Capitalization factor | 18% |

You are required to calculate the brand value.

# Chapter 6 VALUING PRIVATE COMPANIES

6.1 Introduction
6.2 Private Company
6.3 Valuation of Private Companies
6.4 Approaches to Corporate Valuations
6.5 Exercises

## 6.1 INTRODUCTION

The prime goal of a company is to maximize the market volume of equity shares. The market price of a company's share is an index of the performance of the company. It takes into account the present and prospective future earnings per share, risk associated with the business, dividend and retention policies of the company. The valuation of shares and business is required when the merger and acquisitions proposals are under consideration. The purchase consideration is determined on the basis of value of business. The valuation of business may also be made at the time of business alliance, joints venture, employee stock options, wealth tax assessment, purchase of controlling interest, conversion of shares into debentures, pledging of shares as a security to obtain loan. The share of a company is a movable property and it can be transferred from person to person. A share of a company represents a bundle of rights, like right to elect directors, receive right to vote on resolutions placed before the members in a meetings right to receive dividends and so on.

The valuation of a company requires expert knowledge. The value of business depends upon the risk profile of the different classes of business it carries and the intangible assets it possesses. It is not possible to ascertain the value of business accurately but the value has to use his skill, experience and knowledge in determination of fair value of business. The value should consider both the company's fundamentals as well as the industry analysis. The value of a company is determined on the basis of its market price. Company's shares are traded on the stock markets. The wealth of the equity shareholders is represented in the market price of the equity shares. The maximization of utility value of shareholder can be achieved by maximizing their economic welfare. The wealth created is reflected in the market value of shares. The financial decisions may cause to create wealth and it is reflected in market price of the company's share.

## 6.2 PRIVATE COMPANY

The Companies Act, 1956 defines a private company as "A company which restricts: (a) transfer of its shares (b) restricts its member to 50 and (c) it is prohibited from issue of prospectus for issue of shares to the public". Thus, a private company is limited company but it is limited to a certain number of members only. To start a private limited company, minimum two persons are required and the maximum is 50. However, a public limited company requires 7 persons to register but there is no limit on maximum number of members. There is a restriction on transfer of shares of a private limited company because after transfer the maximum number of member should not exceed 50. The private limited company cannot issue prospectus for selling shares to the public. However, it can raise capital by issue of shares to friends, relatives and family members of the promoter. A private limited company can start business immediately after registration but a public limited company can start business only after raising minimum amount of capital by issue of shares to the public. A public limited company has to obtain certificate of "Commencement of business" from the registrar of companies. The basic condition for getting this certificate is raising the minimum subscription, i.e., the minimum amount of share capital required to start the business. The public limited companies share can be listed on the stock exchanges and also traded in the stock market. However, a private limited company's shares cannot be listed and traded on the stock exchanges. Thus, the private limited company's shares will not have market price in the stock exchange.

## 6.3 VALUATION OF PRIVATE COMPANIES

The market price of a share serves as an index of the performance of a company. The shares of a private company are not easily transferable. Hence, the valuation of a private company may not be possible due to lack of market price of its shares. However, the value of an enterprise indicates the net assets as shown in the books of accounts. It is the simplest form of valuation of the business. The net assets valuation is the difference between the assets and liabilities based on their balance sheet values. The capital structure of a company will include both debt and equity capital. The debt capital brings with interest tax shields which have a value in it and it will also impose a different risk profile on the equity. Thus, the equity value of an enterprise is equal to the value of the shareholders claims in the company. It also represents the accumulated market value of all the shares of the company. The following are the different concepts of valuation with reference to a private limited company.

(a) $\text{Value per Share} = \dfrac{\text{Shareholder's Equity}}{\text{Number of Shares Outstanding}}$

(b) Value of Company = Value per Share × No. of Equity Shares Outstanding

The shareholder's equity includes equity share capital, reserves and surplus.

The concept of valuation of business is most complicated process. There are many difficulties in determining the value of business and shares. All the businesses are not alike and interchangeable. Vertical and horizontal integration, globalisation and empowerment focus have all created waves of corporate activity which have rarely had a long-term effect on earnings but had significant effects on their valuation. It is often difficult to separate the value of business from the value of its management. The price paid will always depend on how much of a risk the buyer is prepared to take.

## 6.4 APPROACHES TO CORPORATE VALUATIONS

The fundamental approach to valuation of business assets is the importance of company's fundamentals for its valuation. The following are the broad approaches to appraising the value of a company.

### (a) Adjusted Book Value Approach

The simplest approach to valuing a private company is to rely on the information given on its balance sheet. The book values of the investor claims can be calculated directly. However, the assets may be totalled and from this total non-investor claims can be deducted. This value can be divided by the number of shares outstanding in order to arrive at each investor's claim. The asset's earning power may not be related to its book value hence it is likely to be related to its current replacement cost. The net book value may be substituted by current replacement cost. The most direct approach for calculating the fair market value of the assets on the balance sheet is to find out what they would fetch if the firm were liquidated immediately. However, the accuracy of the book value approach depends on how well the net book values of the company reflects its fair market value. This is due to the inflation, technological changes and organisational capital.

**Illustration 6.1:** The Balance sheet of Hikal Pvt. Ltd. as on 31st March, 2012 is as follows:

**Balance Sheet as on 31.3.2012 (₹ lakhs)**

| Liabilities | ₹ lakhs | Assets | ₹ lakhs |
|---|---|---|---|
| Share capital | 150 | Fixed Assets | 300 |
| Reserve and Surplus | 112 | Investments | 15 |
| Term loan | 30 | **Current Assets:** | |
| Unsecured loan | 13 | Cash and Bank | 10 |
| Current Liabilities | 80 | Debtors | 45 |
| Provisions | 25 | Stock | 30 |
| | | Prepaid-expenses | 5 |
| | | Misc. expenditure | 5 |
| | **410** | | **410** |

You are required to determine the value of the company using adjusted book value approach.

**Solution:**

(a) Value of company using book value approach:

| | | ₹ lakhs |
|---|---|---|
| Fixed Assets | | 300 |
| Investments | | 15 |
| Cash and Bank | | 10 |
| Debtor | | 45 |
| Stock | | 30 |
| Prepaid expenses | | 5 |
| Total | | 405 |
| *Less*: **Current Liabilities and Provisions** | | |
| Current Liabilities | 80 | |
| Provisions | 25 | 105 |
| Value of company | | **300** |

**Note:-** Misc. expenditure is not considered because it has no realisable value.

(b) Value of company using investor's claim approach:

| | ₹ lakhs |
|---|---|
| Share capital | 150 |
| Reserve and Surplus | 112 |
| Term loans | 30 |
| Unsecured loan | 13 |
| Total | 305 |
| *Less*: Misc expenditure | 5 |
| ∴ Value of company | **300** |

**Illustration 6.2:** The following is the summarised Balance sheet of Atul Private Ltd. as on 31[st] March, 2012:

| **Liabilitires** | **₹ lakhs** | **Assets** | **₹ lakhs** |
|---|---|---|---|
| Equity shares (₹ 10 each) | 100 | Fixed Assets | 160 |
| General reserve | 80 | Investments | 40 |
| Profit and Loss A/c | 20 | Stock | 50 |
| Bank loan | 50 | Debtors | 30 |
| Creditors | 30 | Cash | 05 |
| Other Liabilities | 20 | Bank | 15 |
| | **300** | | **300** |

Fixed assets are to be valued at ₹ 150 lakhs. Investments are to be taken at ₹ 42 lakhs. Debtors are bad to the extent of 4%. Interest on loan is payable for 4 months @12% p.a. Stock is valued at ₹ 48.20 lakhs. Calculate the value of Atul Pvt. Ltd.

**Solution: Assets of adjusted value**

| | | ₹ lakhs |
|---|---|---|
| Fixed Assets | | 150.00 |
| Investments | | 42.00 |
| Stock | | 48.20 |
| Debtors | | 28.80 |
| Cash | | 5.00 |
| Bank | | 15.00 |
| Total | | 289.00 |
| *Less*: **Liabilities** | | |
| Creditors | 30 | |
| Other Liabilities | 20 | |
| Interest | 02 | 52.00 |
| Value of company | | **237.00** |

## (b) Direct Comparison Approach

In business, it is a common sense that similar assets should sell at similar prices. Therefore, one can value a business by looking at the price at which a comparable asset has changed hands between a reasonably informed buyer and a reasonably informed seller. This approach is known as direct comparison approach. The following procedure can be applied for calculation of value of a private limited company.

(1) An analysis of the economy for providing the basis for assessing the prospects of various industries.

(2) To analyse the industry to which the subject company belongs.

(3) To carry out an in-depth analysis of the competitive and financial position of the subject company.

(4) To select companies which are similar to the subject company in terms of line of business.

(5) To analyse the financial aspects of the subject company and comparable companies.

(6) To choose the observable financial variable.

(7) Valuation of the subject company.

The key aspects to be covered in the analysis are:

(i) Product portfolio and market segments.

(ii) Cost of inputs.

(iii) Production capacity.

(iv) Market image, distribution reach and customer loyalty.

(v) Product differentiation.

(vi) Managerial competencies.

(vii) Quality of human resources.

(viii) Competitive dynamics.

(ix) Liquidity, leverage and financial position.

(x) Turnover margins and return on investment.

The ratios that are commonly used in direct comparison approach are as follows:

(a) Firm value to PBDIT

(b) Firm value to PBIT

(c) Market-book value

(d) Firm value to book value of assets

**Illustration 6.3:** The following financial information is available for Delta Private Ltd. as on 31-3-2013.

| | **₹ lakhs** |
|---|---|
| Profit before depreciations interest and taxes | 36 |
| Book value of assets | 180 |
| Sales | 250 |

Based on an evaluation of several similar companies in the industry, Alpha, Beta and Gama have been found to be comparable to Delta Private Ltd. The financial information for these companies is as follows:

| Particulars | (₹ lakhs) | | |
|---|---|---|---|
| | **Alpha** | **Beta** | **Gama** |
| PBDIT | 24 | 30 | 40 |
| Book value of assets | 150 | 160 | 200 |
| Sales | 160 | 200 | 320 |
| Market value | 300 | 480 | 720 |
| M.V./PBDIT | 12.5 | 16.0 | 18.0 |
| M.V./Book value | 2.0 | 3.0 | 3.6 |
| M.V./Sales | 1.9 | 2.4 | 2.3 |

Taking into account the characteristics of Delta Private Ltd. and Alpha, Beta and Gama the following multiples appear reasonable for Delta Pvt. Ltd.

MV/PBDIT = 15
MV/Book value = 3
MV/Sales = 2.5

You are required to calculate the value of Delta Pvt. Ltd. using Direct Comparison Approach.

**Solution:**

(i) Calculate of Market value based on PBDIT

$$\therefore \frac{MV}{PBDIT} = 15$$

$$\therefore \text{M.V.} = \text{PBDIT} \times 15$$
$$= 36 \times 15$$
$$= ₹\ 540 \text{ lakhs}$$

(ii) Calculation of Market value based on Book value

$$\therefore \frac{\text{M.V.}}{\text{Book Value}} = 3$$

$$\therefore \text{M.V.} = (\text{B.V.}) \times (3)$$
$$= 180 \times 3$$
$$= ₹\ 540 \text{ lakhs}$$

(iii) Calculation of Market value based on Sales

$$\therefore \frac{\text{M.V.}}{\text{Sales}} = 2.5$$

$$\therefore \text{M.V.} = \text{Sales} \times 2.5$$
$$= ₹\ 250 \times 2.5$$
$$= ₹\ 625 \text{ lakhs}$$

(iv) Calculation of Average market value $= \dfrac{540 + 540 + 625}{3}$

$$= ₹\ \frac{1705}{3} = ₹\ 568.33 \text{ lakhs.}$$

## (c) Discounted Cash Flow Approach

Discounted cash flow approach calls for forecasting cash flows over an indefinite period of time for a private limited company that is expected to grow in future. The valuation of such a company, the investments in fixed assets and net working capital needs to be considered. The cash flow forecast during the explicit forecast period is determined as under:

(i) Select the explicit forecast period
(ii) Define the free cash flow to the firm
(iii) Get a perspective on the driver of free cash flow
(iv) Develop the free cash flow forecast

The free cash flow to the firm is determined as follows:

Free cash flow = Operating free cash flow + Non-operating free cash flow
= NOPAT – Net investment
= Gross cash flow – Gross investments

NOPLAT = Net operating profit less adjusted taxes. It is equal to EBIT less taxes.

EBIT is determined as follows:

| | |
|---|---|
| Profit before tax | xxx |
| + interest expenses | xxx |
| – interest income | xxx |
| – non-operating income | xxx |

Thus, the following steps are used in valuation of a firm:

(i) Forecast the cash flow during the explicit forecast period
(ii) Establish the cost of capital
(iii) Determine the continuing value at the end of the explicit forecast period
(iv) Calculate the value of firm

The value of the firm under discounting cash flow approach is determined as follows:

V = Present value of cash flow during the explicit forecast period
+ Present value of cash flow after the explicit forecast period

**Illustration 6.4:** The financial statements of Zen Pvt. Ltd. are given below:

**(a) Profit and Loss Account**

| | **(₹ lakhs)** | |
|---|---|---|
| | **31.3.11** | **31.3.12** |
| Net sales | 56,000 | 64,400 |
| Other income (Interest) | 1,400 | 2,100 |
| Non-operating income | 700 | 1,400 |
| Total income | 58,100 | 67,900 |
| Cost of goods sold | 32,200 | 37,800 |
| Depreciation | 7,000 | 7,700 |
| Selling and Adm. exp. | 3,500 | 4,200 |

| | | |
|---|---|---|
| Interest | 3,360 | 3,920 |
| Total cost | 46,060 | 53,620 |
| Profit before tax | 12,040 | 14,280 |
| Tax | 3,040 | 4,280 |
| Profit after tax | 9,000 | 10,000 |
| Dividend | 4,000 | 5,600 |
| Retained earnings | 5,000 | 4,400 |

**(b) Balance Sheet**

| | (₹ lakhs) | |
|---|---|---|
| **Liabilities** | | |
| Equity share capital | 21,000 | 21,000 |
| Reserve and Surplus | 16,800 | 21,000 |
| Debt capital | 25,200 | 29,400 |
| | **63,000** | **71,400** |
| **Assets** | | |
| Fixed assets | 42,000 | 45,500 |
| Investments | 12,600 | 14,000 |
| Net current assets | 8,400 | 11,900 |
| | **63,000** | **71,400** |

Required:

(i) What is the EBIT for 2012?

(ii) What is the tax on EBIT for 2012?

(iii) What is the NOPLAT for 2012?

(iv) What is the free cash flow of the company for the year 2012?

(v) Give the break-up of the financing flow for the year 2012?

**Solution:**

(i) EBIT for the year 2012:

| | (₹ lakhs) |
|---|---|
| Profit before tax | 14,280 |
| + Interest paid | 3,920 |
| – Interest income | 2,100 |
| – Non-operating Income | 1,400 |
| EBIT | **14,700** |

(ii) Taxes on EBIT:

| | (₹ lakhs) |
|---|---|
| Tax provisions for the year | 4,280 |
| + Tax yield on interest | 1,176 |
| – Tax on interest income | – 630 |
| – Tax on non-operating income | – 420 |
| Taxes on EBIT | **4,406** |

(iii) NOPAT for the year 2012:

| | (₹ lakhs) |
|---|---|
| EBIT | 14,700 |
| – Tax | 4,406 |
| NOPAT | **10,294** |

(iv) FCFF for the year 2012:

| | (₹ lakhs) |
|---|---|
| NOPAT | 10,294 |
| – Net investment | 7,000 |
| + Non-operating cash flow | 630 |
| | **3,924** |

Net Investment = (45,500 + 11,900 – 42,000 + 8,400)

(v) Break-up of the financial flow is as follows:

| | (₹ lakhs) |
|---|---|
| After tax interest expense | 2,744 |
| + Cash dividend | 5,600 |
| – Net borrowing | 4,200 |
| + Excess investments | 1,400 |
| – After tax income on excess marketable securities | 1,470 |
| Total | **4,074** |

**Note:** Tax rate is approx 30%.

**Illustration 6.5:** DCM Pvt. Ltd. has employed a total capital of ₹ 100 lakh, provided equally by 10% debt and equity shares of ₹ 100 each. Its cost of equity is 14 per cent and it is subject to corporate tax rate of 40%. The projected free cash flows to all investors for 5 years are as follows:

| Year End | ₹ lakhs |
|---|---|
| 1 | 30 |
| 2 | 20 |
| 3 | 50 |
| 4 | 15 |
| 5 | 60 |

You are requested to compute:

(a) Value of the Company and

(b) Valuation from the perspective of equity investors assuming 10% debt is repayable at the year end and interest is paid at the end of each year.

**Solution:**

(i) Computation of weighted average cost of capital

| Source | After Tax Cost (%) | Weight | Total Cost (%) |
|---|---|---|---|
| Equity | 14 | 0.5 | 7.00 |
| Debt | 6 | 0.5 | 3.00 |
| WACC | | | **10.00** |

Cost of debt after tax = 10 (1 – 0.4) = 6%

(a) Valuation of firm based on cost of capital

| Year | FCFF (₹ lakhs) | P.V. Factor @10% | Present Value (₹ lakhs) |
|---|---|---|---|
| 1 | 30 | 0.909 | 27.27 |
| 2 | 20 | 0.826 | 16.52 |
| 3 | 50 | 0.751 | 37.55 |
| 4 | 15 | 0.683 | 10.25 |
| 5 | 60 | 0.621 | 37.26 |
| Present value of cash inflow | | | 128.85 |
| *Less*: Present value of debt | | | 50.00 |
| Value of equity | | | **78.85** |

(b) Valuation of the firm based on Investors Perspective

| Year | FCFF to all Investors (₹ lakhs) | After tax payment for Debt holders | FCFF to Shareholders | PV Factor @14% | Total PV (₹ lakhs) |
|---|---|---|---|---|---|
| 1 | 30 | 3 | 27 | 0.877 | 23.68 |
| 2 | 20 | 3 | 17 | 0.769 | 13.07 |
| 3 | 50 | 3 | 47 | 0.675 | 31.72 |
| 4 | 15 | 3 | 12 | 0.592 | 7.10 |
| 5 | 60 | 53 | 7 | 0.519 | 3.63 |
| Total present value | | | | | **79.20** |

Interest on ₹ 50 lakhs @10% = ₹ 5 lakhs

∴ After tax payment to = 5(1 – 0.4)

Debt holders = ₹ 3 lakhs

**Illustration 6.6:** RPF Pvt. Ltd. is a growing company. Its free cash flows for equity holders (FCFE) have been growing at a rate of 20% in recent years. This growth rate is expected to continue for another 5 years. The FCFE are likely to grow at the normal rate of 8 per cent. The required rate of return on the shares by the investors is 15 per cent. The company's weighted average cost of capital is 10 per cent. The amount of FCFE per share as the beginning of the current year is ₹ 20. Determine the value per share based on free cash flow approach.

**Solution:**

Calculation of present value of FCFE (1-5 year)

| Year | FCFE Per Share | P.V. Factor @15% | Total P.V. |
|---|---|---|---|
| 1 | $20(1 + 0.20)^1 = 24$ | 0.870 | 20.88 |
| 2 | $20(1 + 0.20)^2 = 28.8$ | 0.756 | 21.77 |
| 3 | $20(1 + 0.20)^3 = 34.56$ | 0.658 | 22.74 |
| 4 | $20(1 + 0.20)^4 = 41.47$ | 0.572 | 23.72 |
| 5 | $20(1 + 0.20)^5 = 49.76$ | 0.497 | 24.73 |
| Total FCFE | | | **113.84** |

$$\text{Value of Share} = \frac{FCFE_6}{K_e - g}.$$

where

FCFE = free cash flow to equity holders

$K_e$ = required of rate of return

g = growth rate in cash flow

$$\therefore V = \frac{49.76\,(1.08)}{15\% - 8\%} = \frac{53.74}{0.07} = ₹\,767.71$$

$$\therefore \text{Present Value} = 767.7 \times 0.497$$
$$= ₹\,381.55$$
$$\therefore \text{Maximum Value} = ₹\,381.55 + ₹\,113.84$$
$$\text{Per Share} = ₹\,495.39$$

**Illustration 6.7**: Determine the continuing value of the firm with the help of the following information:

| | **(₹ lakhs)** |
|---|---|
| Cash flow from business operations at the end of explicit forecast period (year 6) | 560 |
| Investment required in capital expenditure and current assets during year 6 | 120 |
| Expected annual growth rate in free cash flow, after forecast period | 10% |
| Weighted average cost of capital | 12% |
| Cost of equity capital | 15% |

**Solution:**

Determination of present value with respect to continuing value

$$CV_6 = \frac{FCFF_7}{WACC - g}$$

where

$CV_6$ = continuing value at the end of $6^{th}$ year

$FCFF_7$ = free cash flow to all investors at the end of $7^{th}$ year

WACC = Weighted average cost of capital

g = Growth rate in free cash flow

$$\therefore CV_6 = \frac{440(1.08)}{12\% - 10\%} = \frac{475.2}{2\%} = ₹\,23{,}760 \text{ lakhs}$$

$$\therefore CV_6 = 23{,}760 \text{ lakhs} \times \text{P.V. Factor @}12\% \text{ for 6 year}$$

$$\therefore CV_6 = 23{,}760 \times 0.507$$
$$= ₹\,1{,}246 \text{ lakhs}$$

**Note:** $FCFF_7$ = Gross Cash Flow – Investment in Capital Expenditure and Current Assets

= ₹ 560 lakhs – 120 lakhs

= ₹ 440 lakhs

### (d) Earnings Based Approach

Earnings approach is guided by the economic proposition that business valuation should be related to the firm's potential of future earnings or cash flow generating capacity. Earnings can be expressed in the sense of accounting as well as financial management. Earnings approach is based on the two parameters, the earnings of the firm and capitalisation rate applicable to such earnings in the market. Earnings are the normal expected annual profits. There is an explicit need for marketing adjustments to the profit of the last years. In order to arrive at credible future maintainable profits, extraordinary items of income as well as expense are to be adjusted. It is also necessary to understand the profit of the business focusing on identifying the major growth and income drivers. Additional income expected in the coming years should also be considered. While valuing the firm, the valuer should try to familiarise himself with all major factors that had affected the profits of the business in the past years and are likely to affect them in the future years.

The risk return framework of financial decision making, warrant a higher capitalisation factor, similarly, businesses carrying a low degree of risk are subject to lower capitalisation factor. The risk factors to be considered are sales, earnings, degree of operating leverage, degree of financial leverage, nature and extent of competition, availability of substitutes and their prices, change in technology and the level of government regulations. There are number of internal as well as external factors associated with a business that can influence the risk and capitalisation factor.

Normally the capitalisation factor for a business firm should be higher than that of a government security. It should match around the firms operating in similar type of business. There can be convincing reasons for using different capitalisation rates. Firms using the potential and prospects of achieving abnormal growth rates and other firms in the industry managed by a well known management team can have low capitalisation factor. The value of business of a private limited company can be determined as under.

$$V = \frac{\text{Furture Maintainable Profits}}{\text{Capitalisation Factor}}.$$

Future maintainable profits can be determined on the basis of average profit for the past few years after adjusting extraordinary items and the capitalisation factor can be used based on the relevant factor of the company business.

**Illustration 6.8:** Alok Pvt. Ltd. has reported a profit of ₹ 70 lakhs after paying taxes @30 per cent. The analyst ascertains that the current year's income includes:

(a) Extraordinary income of ₹ 10 lakhs.

(b) Extraordinary loss of ₹ 3 lakhs.

Apart from existing operations which are normal in nature and are likely to continue in future the company expects to launch a new product in the coming year. Revenue and cost estimates of the new product are as follows:

| | **₹ lakhs** |
|---|---|
| Sales | 400 |
| Cost of materials | 150 |
| Cost of labour | 100 |
| Fixed costs (Allocated) | 50 |
| Additional fixed costs | 30 |

You are required to compute the value of business assuming the capitalisation rate applicable to such business in the market is 15%.

**Solution:**

(a) Calculate of future maintainable profits

| | | **(₹ lakhs)** |
|---|---|---|
| Profit before tax | | 100 |
| (₹ 70 lakh (1 – 0.30) | | |
| *Less*: Extraordinary income | | 10 |
| *Add*: Extraordinary loss | | 3 |
| *Add*: **Incremental income** | | |
| Sales | 400 | |
| – Material | 150 | |
| –Labour | 100 | |
| –Add. fixed cost | 30 | 120 |
| ∴ Expected profit before tax | | 213 |
| *Less*: Taxes @30% | | 63.90 |
| Future maintainable profit | | **149.10** |

(b) Calculation of value of business

$$V = \frac{\text{Future Maintainable Profit}}{\text{Capitalisation Rate}}$$

$$= \frac{149.10}{0.15} = ₹\,994\text{ lakhs}$$

**Illustration 6.9:** Caran Pvt. Ltd. is expecting an annual EBIT of ₹ 1,00,000. The company has ₹ 4 lakhs Debt at 10% interest. The cost of equity capitalisation rate is 12.5%. You are required to calculate the total value of the company and overall cost of capital.

**Solution:**

(a) Calculation of net income/earnings

| | |
|---|---|
| EBIT | ₹ 1,00,000 |
| – Interest | 40,000 |
| Net earnings | **60,000** |

(b) Calculation of value of equity

$$V_e = \frac{\text{Earnings (FMP)}}{\text{Capitalisation Rate}}$$

$$= \frac{60.000}{12.5\%} = ₹\,4,80,000$$

(c) Value of Firm = Value of Equity + Value of Debt

= ₹ 4,80,000 + 4,00,000

= ₹ 8,80,000

(d) Calculation of overall cost of capital $= \dfrac{\text{EBIT}}{\text{Value of Firm}}$

$$= ₹\frac{1,00,000}{8,80,000} \times 100 = 11.36\%$$

**Illustration 6.10:** The operating income of C Pvt. Ltd. is ₹ 6,00,000. The firm's cost of debt is 10%. The amount of debt is ₹ 15,00,000. The overall cost of capital is 15%. You are required to determine:

(i) Total value of firm

(ii) Cost of equity.

**Solution:**

(i) Calculation of net earnings

| | |
|---|---|
| EBIT | ₹ 6,00,000 |
| – Interest on debt | 1,50,000 |
| Net earnings | **4,50,000** |

(ii) Value of firm $\dfrac{\text{EBIT}}{K_e}$

where,

EBIT means earning before interest and taxes

$K_e$ = overall cost of capital

$$\therefore V = \frac{6,00,000}{15\%} = ₹40,00,000$$

(iii) Calculation of cost of equity

$$\text{Cost of equity } (K_e) = \frac{\text{Net Earnings}}{\text{Value of Equity}}$$

where,

$K_e$ = Cost of equity

$$\therefore V_e = \frac{4,50,000}{25,00,000} = 18\%.$$

**Note:** Value of Equity = Total value of firm – Value of debt

= ₹ 40,00,000 – 15,00,000

= ₹ 25,00,000

## (e) Dividend Approach

The fundamental approach to valuation of business is the importance of company's fundamentals for its valuation. The important approaches for corporate valuation are as follows:

(i) Dividend Approach

(ii) Dividend Growth Approach

These approaches help to ascertain the company's value on the basis of financial information that is relevant to company and its future.

The dividend capitalisation model is the basis of share valuation model. However, the value of an equity share can simply be determined by capitalising the expected earnings of the company. When the earnings of the company are stable both the growth rate and retention rate will be zero. In such a case the earnings rate and dividend rate will be the same. The following formula can be used to determine the value of a share:

$$V_o = \frac{E_1}{K_e}$$

where,

$E_1$ is expected earning per share
$K_e$ = capitalisation rate
$V_o$ = current value of equity share

In case of dividend growth approach the value of a share is determined as follows:

$$V = D_0 \frac{(1+g)}{(k-g)}$$

where,

V = value of a share
$D_o$ = current dividend
g = growth rate in dividend
k = Required rate of return
(or capitalisation rate)

**Illustration 6.11:** 'S' Pvt. Ltd. provides you the following information:

EPS = ₹ 12
Capitalization Rate = 15%
Retained Earnings = Nil

Calculate the price of an equity share according to dividend capitalisation approach.

**Solution:**

Retained Earnings is nil. It means dividend per share will be ₹ 12.

$$\therefore V = \frac{E_1}{K_e} = \frac{12}{0.15} = ₹\,80$$

**Illustration 6.12:** As per financial records of Dhamdasani Pvt. Ltd. dividend @20% was paid in the last year. The paid up capital of the company is ₹ 6,00,000 divided into shares of ₹ 10 each. Operating profit is ₹ 4,00,000. The tax rate is 30%. The company expects a growth rate of 5% in dividend. The capitalisation rate is 10%. Determine the value of a share and value of company based on:

(a) Dividend Approach
(b) Dividend Growth Approach
(c) Earnings Approach

**Solution:**

(a) Divided Approach

$$V = \frac{E_1}{K_e} = \frac{2}{10\%} = ₹\,20$$

Value of firm (Equity) = value per share × No. of share

= ₹ 20 × 60,000

= ₹ 12,00,000

(b) Dividend Growth Approach

$$V = D_o \frac{(1+g)}{k-g}$$

$$= \frac{2\,(1.05)}{0.10-0.05}$$

$$= \frac{2.10}{0.05} = ₹\,42$$

Value of firm (Equity) = ₹ 42 × 60,000

= 25,20,000

(c) Earnings Approach

Calculation of Earnings

| | ₹ |
|---|---|
| Operating profit | 4,00,000 |
| *Less*: Tax @30% | 1,20,000 |
| Earnings | **2,80,000** |

$$\therefore \text{EPS} = \frac{2,80,000}{60,000} = ₹\,4.67$$

$$\therefore V = \frac{\text{EPS}}{K_e} = \frac{4.67}{10} = ₹\,46.70$$

Value of firm (Equity) = 46.70 × 60,000

= ₹ 28,02,000

## 6.5 EXERCISES

1. What is a private limited company? What are the restrictions on private limited company under the Companies Act, 1956?
2. How can you determine the value of a private limited company?
3. What is adjusted book value approach of valuation of a firm?
4. Explain the direct comparison approach to valuation of a firm?
5. What is discounted cash flow approach?
6. Write short notes on the following:
   (a) Direct Comparison Approach
   (b) Discounted Cash Flow Approach
   (c) Free Cash Flow
   (d) Dividend Approach
   (e) Earnings Approach
7. Veena Pvt. Ltd. is expected to pay a dividend of ₹ 2 per share of ₹ 10 each. The dividend is expected to grow at 5%. The current capitalisation rate is 12.0%. You are required to find out value of equity share of the company.
8. Diwan Private Ltd. has reported a profit of ₹ 65 lakh, after paying taxes @35 per cent. The analyst ascertains that the current year's income includes an extraordinary income of ₹ 10 lakhs and extraordinary loss of ₹ 3 lakh. The existing operations are likely to be continued in future and the company expects to launch a new product in the coming year. Revenue and cost estimates in respects of the new product are as follows:

| | **₹ lakhs** |
|---|---|
| Sales | 60 |
| Materials | 15 |
| Labour | 10 |
| Allocated fixed cost | 5 |
| Additional fixed cost | 8 |

   You are required to compute the value of business assuming that capitalistion rate applicable to similar business in the market is 15 per cent.
   (Answer: ₹ 520 lakhs)

(9) Chinatown Private Ltd. is a growing company. Its free cash flows for equity holder (FCFE) have been growing at a rate of 25 per cent in recent year. This growth is expected to continue for 5 years and then the FCFE is likely to grow at the normal rate of 8 per cent. The required rate of return on these shares is 15 per cent. The company's weighted average cost of capital is 12 per cent. The amount of FCFE per share at the beginning of the current year is ₹ 30. Determine the value of share based on free cash flow approach.
   (Answer: ₹ 194 + ₹ 702 = ₹ 896)

10. Mohan Private Ltd. has estimated the following parameters:

| | |
|---|---|
| Free cash flow at the end of 9th year | ₹ 17.6 lakhs |
| Growth rate in cash flow | 10% |
| Weighted average cost of capital | 14% |

   You are required to find out the continuing value of the company.
   (Answer: ₹ 440 lakhs)

11. The data related to Ashoka Pvt. Ltd. is given below:

| | (₹ lakhs) | | | | | |
|---|---|---|---|---|---|---|
| **Year** | **3** | **4** | **5** | **6** | **7** | **8** |
| Profit after tax | 24 | 29 | 28 | 32 | 38 | 40 |
| Fixed assets (Net) | 190 | 220 | 240 | 266 | 294 | 324 |
| Investments | 20 | 10 | – | – | – | – |
| Net current assets | 70 | 75 | 88 | 90 | 100 | 109 |
| Debt | 129 | 140 | 150 | 161 | 177 | 192 |

You are required to calculate FCFE for the explicit forecast period.

(Answer: ₹ (lakhs) 15, 15, 15, 16 and 16)

12. The projected free cash flow of Awaz Pvt. Ltd. for the year 7 is ₹ 1,178 lakhs. Therefore, it is expected to grow at a constant rate of 14 per cent per year. You are required to calculate expected continuing value at the end of 7th year.

(Answer: ₹ 44,764 lakhs)

# Chapter 7 OPTION PRICING APPLICATIONS IN VALUATION

7.1 Introduction
7.2 Options
7.3 Important Terms Used in Options
7.4 Types of Options
7.5 Option Valuation
7.6 Binominal Model for Option Values
7.7 Black-Scholes Model for Option Values
7.8 Exercises

## 7.1 INTRODUCTION

There is a risk in every financial decision. Assessing risk and incorporating the same in the final decision is an integral part of financial analysis. To estimate the risk-adjusted discount rate, we should be able to measure and price financial risk. The financial managers have to deal with various types of risks. The derivatives market performs a number of economic functions. Price in an organised derivatives market reflects the perception of the market participants about the future and lead the prices of underlying to the perceived future level. The prices of derivatives coverage with the prices of the underlying at the expiration of the derivatives contract. Thus, derivatives help in the discovery of the future as well as current prices. Derivative contracts have several variations. The most common variants are forwards, futures and options. Three broad categories of participants, i.e., hedges, speculators and arbitrageurs trade in the derivatives market. Hedgers face risk associated with the price of an asset. They use futures or options markets to reduce or eliminate the risk.

Options belong to a broader class of assets called contingent claims. There can be as many different options contracts as the number of items to buy or sell. Stock options, commodity options foreign exchange options and interest rate options are traded on organised exchanges. An options buyer has the right but not the obligation to exercise on the seller. The worst that can happen to a buyer is the loss of the premium paid by him. His downside is limited to the premium, but his upside is potentially unlimited. This optionality has a value expressed in terms of the option price. It is the supply and demand in the secondary market that derives the price of an option. There are various models that help to get close to the true price of an option. The most popular model for pricing options is the Black-Scholes model. It was published in 1973 where the Chicago Board of Options Exchange was set up.

## 7.2 OPTIONS

Option is a contract that confers to its holder/owner the right to buy or sell a specified security at a specified price on or before a given date. However, there is no such obligation on the holder. It is a special contract under which the option holder enjoys the right to buy or sell something without the obligation to do so. Options belong to a broader class assets known as contingent. It is an asset whose pay-off in future depends on the outcome of some uncertain event. Options belong to the derivative securities. The buyer of the option is placed in an advantageous situation as he will exercise his option only when it is profitable to him. On the other hand, the seller of the option is in disadvantageous position as he is under obligation to buy or sell the securities in case the buyer exercises his option. In operational terms, the seller of the option runs the risk of loss for assuming which he charges option premium from the buyer of the option.

## 7.3 IMPORTANT TERMS USED IN OPTIONS

The following are the important term associated with the options:

(i) **Call option:** The option to buy is called call option.

(ii) **Put option:** The option to sell is known as put option.

(iii) **Option holder:** The buyer of the option is called an option holder.

(iv) **Option writer:** The seller of the option is known as option writer.

(v) **Striking price:** The fixed price at which the option holder can buy or sell the underlying asset is called as striking price.

(vi) **Option price:** The price the option buyer pays to the option seller is called as option price. It is also called as option premium.

(vii) **Maturity date:** The date when the option expires or matures is known as the expiration or maturity date.

(viii) **Exercising option:** The act of buying or selling the underlying asset as per the option contract is known as exercising the option.

(ix) **ATM:** At the money option is an option that would lead to zero cash flow to the holder if it were exercised immediately.

(x) **ITM:** In the money option is an option that would lead to a positive cash flow to the holder if it were exercised immediately.

(xi) **OTM:** Out of the money option is an option that would lead to a negative cash flow to the holder if it were exercised immediately.

Exchange trade options are standardised in terms of quantity, trading cycle, expiration date, strike price type of option and mode of settlement. Option contracts on individual securities on the National Stock Exchange are in the multiples of 100 and have a maximum of three months trading cycle. These options shall expire on the last Thursday of the month and shall have five strike prices stipulated by the exchange as per American style and settled in cash.

## 7.4 TYPES OF OPTIONS

There are two types of options. One is call option and the other is put option.

**Call Option:** The call option is a contract that gives the holder the right but not the obligation to buy specified securities at a specified price on or before a specified exercise date. American options are more flexible in nature because they can be exercised at any time up to the expiration date. On the other hand, European options can be exercised only on the maturity date. The call option buyers expect the price of securities to go up hence they are bullish.

**Put Option:** A put option is just opposite of a call option. As put options gives the holder the right but not the obligation to sell securities, on or by a certain date at a fixed exercise price. Thus, the writer of the put option has the obligation to buy securities in the case the put owner decides to exercise his option. The put option writer is at the receiving end, he receives the put premium from the put buyer. The put option sellers expect the price of securities to go down and therefore they are bearish. In case of the decrease in price, the call buyer does not buy the securities because the prevailing share price is less than the exercise price. In such a situation the call writer gains equivalent to the option premium he has received at the time of selling the call option.

## 7.5 OPTION VALUATION

The call option buyer expects the price of securities to go up so that he can be benefited. The reverse is the case of call writer. He expects the price of security to fall so that he can be benefited. If the price decreases, the call buyer does not buy the securities and the call writer gains equivalent to the option premium he has received at the time of selling the call option. Thus, it can be deduced that the value of call option is either zero or positive. It cannot be negative as it implies that the call holder buys the security at a price which is higher than the market price of the share. Thus, the value of call option on its expiration date will be as follows:

$$C_l = \max(S_l - E_l\ 0)$$

where

$C_l$ = value of call option

$S_l$ = share price

$E_l$ = exercise price

$\max(S_l - E_l)$ implies the maximum value which is either zero or higher.

A put option gives the holder the right but not the obligation to sell securities on or by a certain date at a fixed exercise price. Thus, the writer of the put option has the obligation to buy securities in case the put owner decides to exercise his option. The put option writer is at the receiving end, he receives the put premium down the put buyer. The put option holder will exercise his right to sell the securities if the price of the securities fall bellow the exercise price (E) at the date of expiration. In case $S_l$ is greater than $E_l$ he will prefer to sell at a higher price in the market than to sell to the put option writer.

### 7.5.1 Call Option Boundries

There can be moved to demand for call option till such time there is an upward revision of the option price. Therefore, to prevent arbitrage the value of the call today must be either greater than or equal to the difference of the share price today and the exercise price. Thus, it can be deduced that the call options which have still some time to run have their lower bound either zero or $S_O - E_l$ whichever is higher. The lower bound determines the intrinsic value of the call option. Intrinsic value of a call is the amount of option is in the money that is the excess of share price over exercise price. It is out of money, that is, exercise price is higher than the share price, its intrinsic value is zero. On the other hand, the time value of an option is the difference between the option premium and its intrinsic value. The longer the time to expiration the greater is an options time value. At expiration an option would have no time value. The highest value of the call option can never be more than the price of the share itself. This is the upper bound. This value can be reached only if the option has a very long time to expiration or is not, likely to be exercised until far into the future. In these situations the present value of the strike price to be paid in very distant future reproaches zero. As a result the value of the call option approaches the value of share. However in a practical situation, the call option price is likely to be in the shaded region. The upper bound is more a theoritical possibility. It is because the share and the call option have the same price, everyone will rush to sell the call option and buy the share. It is more likely to be an upward–sloping line or more close to the lower bound.

### 7.5.2 Factors Influencing Option Valuation

The option value depends upon the following five key factors:

(i) **Exercise price:** The higher the exercise price, the lower the value of the call option.

(ii) **Expiration date:** The longer the time to expiration date, the more valuable is the call option.

(iii) **Strike price:** The value of call option increases with the stock price increase.

(iv) **Variability of the stock price:** Call option has value when there is a possibility that the stock price exceeds the exercise price before the expiration date. Thus, the higher the variability of the stock price, the greater will be the likelihood that the stock price will exceed the exercise price.

(v) **Interest rate:** The payment of exercise price is payable when he exercises the call option. The payment is made in future. Thus, higher the interest rate, the greater the benefit will be from delayed payment. The value of call option is positively related to the interest rate.

(vi) **Current share price:** The share price prevailing in the market has a positive impact on the call option value. Thus, the higher the current market price, the higher will be the value of a call option.

(vii) **Dividends:** The option premium on contract also depends upon dividend payment. Companies paying high dividends may not be volatile. The prospective buyers avoid such stocks. Option writers collect the dividends in addition to their premium income, they naturally prefer to write options on high dividend stocks. The buyers and sellers have to compromise, the premium lowers for high-dividend paying stocks.

**Illustration 7.1:** An investor is interested in buying a call option on Tata Motors to be exercised after two years, with exercise price of ₹ 200. The share is sold at ₹ 180. The investor expects the price of Tata Motors after two years, to be either ₹ 210 or ₹ 240. The risk-free interest rate is 6%. What will be the expected values of option prices at the end of two years?

**Solution:**

(i) $C_1 = \max(S_1 - E_1 0)$

where $S_1 =$ ₹ 210

$\therefore C_1 =$ ₹ 210 – 200

= ₹ 10

when $S_1 = 240$

$C_1 =$ ₹ 240 – 200

= ₹ 40

**Illustration 7.2:** The share of Maruti Ltd. is quoted at ₹ 120. After 6 months, its price will be either ₹ 150 with probability of 0.8 or ₹ 110 with probability of 0.20. An European call option exists with an exercise piece of ₹ 130. What will be the expected value of call option price at the maturity date?

**Solution:**

Expected Value of call option:

| Expected Share Price ₹ | Exercise Price ₹ | Call Value ₹ | Probability | Expected Call Value |
|---|---|---|---|---|
| 110 | 130 | 0 | 0.2 | 0 |
| 150 | 130 | 20 | 0.8 | 16 |
| Expected call value | | | | **16** |

**Illustration 7.3:** The market price of a share is ₹ 260 and the exercise price of a call option is ₹ 15. Find out the intrinsic value of the option and the time value of the option.

**Solution:**

(i) Intrinsic value of option = ₹ 260 – ₹ 250
= ₹ 10

(ii) Time value of option = ₹ 15 – ₹ 10
= ₹ 5.

**Illustration 7.4:** An investor is interested in buying a call option to purchase RIL to be exercised after one year with an exercise price of ₹ 130. The current market price of the share is ₹ 125. The risk free rate of interest is 7%. You are required to find the value of investment when (a) the shares are purchased and (b) when call options are purchased assuming that the price of RIL will be either ₹ 140 or ₹ 160 after one year.

**Solution:**

(a) When call value is ₹ 10

| | |
|---|---|
| Compounded value $E/(1 \cdot R_1)^+$<br>(130 × 1.07) or (130 × 0.935) | 121.55 |
| ∴ Compounded value of ₹ 121.55 invested at 7% | ₹ 130 |
| + Call value | 10 |
| Value of investment | **140** |

(b) When call value is ₹ 30

| | |
|---|---|
| Compounded value as above | ₹ 130 |
| + Call value | 30 |
| Value of investment | **160** |

### 7.5.3 Value of Call and Put

Though the quoted price of a put or call is affected by many factors, the most important variable is the **market price behaviour of the underlying equity**. It derives any significant move in the price of the option and also determines its profit potential. Thus, when the underlying stock moves up in the price of the option and also determines its profit potential. Thus, when the underlying stock moves up in the price, **calls do well**. On the other hand, when the price of the underlying stock drops, put do well. Thus, the fundamental value of a put or call depends on the exercise price stated on the option and the prevailing market price of the underlying. Therefore, the value of a call is determined on the basis of the following formula.

$$\text{Value of call} = \left\{ \begin{matrix}\text{Market price of} \\ \text{underlying equity}\end{matrix} - \begin{matrix}\text{Striking price} \\ \text{in the call}\end{matrix} \right\} \times 100$$

$$\therefore V = (MP - SPC) \times 100$$

In other words, the fundamental value of a call is the difference between the market price and the strike price it indicates that a call has a value whenever the market price of the underlying equity exceeds the strike price stipulated on the call. For example, a call carrying a strike price of ₹ 60 on an equity presently trading at ₹ 70 has a value of ₹ 1,000 a s follows:

$$V = (MP - SPC) \times 100$$
$$= (70 - 60) \times 100$$
$$= ₹\ 1{,}000$$

On the other hand, a **Put** cannot be valued in the same way because puts and calls allow the holder to do different things. A reverse order of the above equation can be used to find out the value of a **Put** as follows:

$$\text{Value of Put} = \left( \begin{matrix}\text{Striking price} \\ \text{of put}\end{matrix} - \begin{matrix}\text{Market price of the} \\ \text{underlying equity}\end{matrix} \right) \times 100$$

$$\therefore V = (SPP - MP) \times 100$$

Thus, a put has a value so long as the market price of the underlying asset is less than the strike price stipulated on the put.

When a call has a strike price that is less than the market price of the underlying equity, it has a positive value which is known as an **in-the-money option**. When the strike price exceeds the market price of the underlying equity, the call has no real value and it is known as an **out of the money option**. As the option has no intrinsic value, its price is made up solely of investment premium.

**Illustration 7.5:** Equity shares of C Ltd. are currently sold at ₹ 90 per share. Both the call option and put option for a period of 3 months are available for ₹ 3 per share and ₹ 2 per share respectively. An investor wants to create a straddle position in this share. Find out his net pay off the expiration of the option period, if the share price on that day happens to be ₹ 90 or ₹ 106.

**Solution:**

A straddle position means the investor will buy both the call option as well as the put option and pay the premium on both. The net pay-off position may be as follows:

Total Premium Paid = ₹ 3 + ₹ 2 = ₹ 5.

If the share price happens to be ₹ 90 the call option will not be exercised. Thus, pay-off will be equal to:

Pay-off on put – Premium paid = ₹ (97 – 90) – 5
= ₹ 7 – 5
= ₹ 2.

If the share price happens to be ₹ 106, the put option will not be exercised. Hence, the net pay-off will be equal to:

Pay-off on call – Premium paid = ₹ (106 – 97) – ₹ 5
= ₹ 9 – ₹ 5
= ₹ 4.

The investor will be benefited where the price is less than or more than the strike price on the expiry data.

## 7.6 BINOMIAL MODEL FOR OPTION VALUES

Binomial model is based on the assumption that there are only two possible prices for the share at the end of the period. It is a continuous time model in the limit. It is possible to construct a risk-free hedged portfolio by buying shares and writing call options on the shares. As the resulting portfolio is risk-free, it would be expected that only a risk-free rate of return would be obtained. This enables the investors to obtain a value for the call option. The formula for the value of a call option with one period to expiry can be written as follows:

$$V_c = H\left(P_0 - \frac{P_1}{1+r}\right)$$

where

$V_c$ = the value of the call option with one period to expiry
r = risk free rate of interest
$P_0$ = current share price
$P_l$ = lower value of the share at the end period

$$H = \frac{V_u - V_l}{P_u - P_l} = \text{Hedging Ratio}$$

$V_u$ is the upper value of the option at the end of the period
$V_l$ is the lower value of the option at the end of the period
$P_u$ is the upper value of the share at the end of the period

In the binomial option price formula, it is required to value a call one period before expiration given the following information:

Present price of the share ₹ 10,
Exercise price of call option ₹ 10,
Risk-free interest 25%.

Assume that the share price will either increase to ₹ 15 or decrease to ₹ 5 by the exercise date. It is possible to construct a fully hedged position by buying shares and writing call option as follows:

**Cash Flows in Fully Hedged Position Flows at T**

| | | Possible Share Prices | |
|---|---|---|---|
| | **Flows at 10** | **₹ 15** | **₹ 5** |
| Buy one share | –10 | 15 | 5 |
| Write two calls | +2C | –10 | – |
| | | 5 | 5 |

The cash flows at the beginning of the period and the end of the period when one share is purchased and two calls written are shown in the above table. It is observed that at the end of the period, the net outcome is same irrespective of whether the ₹ 15 price of ₹ 5 price prevails in the market. The reason is that if the share price at the end of the period is ₹ 15, then the share purchased will be worth ₹ 15, while the holder of the call written will required two shares to be delivered for which ₹ 20 will be paid. These shares will have to be purchased in the market at the price of ₹ 15 each and the total cost of ₹ 30 giving a loss of ₹ 10. If the price of the exercise date is ₹ 5, then the value of the one share held will be ₹ 5 and the call will go unexercised and will have a value of zero. This is because the strategy results in a certain outcome whichever possible share price results, the return on the strategy should be certain i.e. the risk-free rate of return. Therefore, we can say:

$$(10 - 2c)\ 1.25 = 5$$

or $$12.50 - 2.5c = 5$$

or $$2.5c = 7.5$$

$$\therefore \quad c = 3$$

Thus, it can be observed form the above equation that investors have a net investment of ₹ 4, i.e., the cost of one share minus the premium received on writing two calls and as the outcome of this investment is certain, investors would expect to earn the risk free rate of return. In this case investors require one share for every two calls written. The share to-option ratio is called the hedge ratio option date. In this example, the option date is 0.5.

**Illustration 7.6:** The following data are related to Prakash Industries Ltd.:

$S = 200, \quad u = 1.4, \quad d = 0.9$

$E = 220, \quad r = 0.10, \quad R = 1.10$

$c_u = \max(u_s - E_1\ 0) = \max(280 - 220, 0) = 60$

$c_d = \max(d_s - E_1\ 0) = \max(180 - 220, 0) = 0.$

You are required determine the value of A and B, and then determine the value of call option.

**Solution:**

(a) Value of A and B can be calculated as follows:

$$A = \frac{c_u - c_d}{(u-d)s} = \frac{60}{0.5\,(200)} = 0.6$$

$$B = \frac{d\,(c_d - {}_u c_d)}{(u-d)R} = \frac{0.9\,(60)}{0.5\,(1.10)} = -98.18$$

The portfolio consists of 0.6 of a share plus borrowing of 98.18 which entails a repayment of 98.18(1.1) = ₹ 108 after one year.

(b) The value of call option will be determined as follows:

| Portfolio | Call Optional |
|---|---|
| When u occurs (1.4 × 200 × 0.6 – 108) = 60 | $c_u = 60$ |
| When d occurs (0.9 × 200 × 0.6 – 108 = 0 | $c_d = 0$ |

Give the equivalence of the call option and the portfolio, the value of call option:

$$C = AS - B = 0.6 \times 200 - 98.18$$

$$= ₹\ 120 - 98.18$$

$$= ₹\ 21.82.$$

## 7.7 BLACK-SCHOLES MODEL FOR OPTION VALUES

This model has developed by Fisher Black and Myron Scholes it is a precise model used to determine the equilibrium value of an options. It is widely used in options pricing. It provides rich insight into the valuation of debt relation to equity. It is based on the following assumptions:

1. There are no transaction costs and taxes.
2. The risk form interest rate is constant.
3. The market operates continuously.
4. There is no dividend payment on shares.
5. The share price move continuously either upwards or downwards.
6. The options are exercised only at maturity.
7. Shares can be sold short without penalty and short sellers receive the full proceeds from the transaction.

The equilibrium value of an option can be determined as follows:

$$V_c = P_s\,(Nd_1) - \frac{P_x}{e\,(RF)\,(T)} \times Nd_2$$

$$d_1 = \frac{I_n\left(\frac{P_s}{P_x}\right) + T\left(RF + \frac{\sigma^2}{2}\right)}{\sigma\sqrt{T}}$$

$$d_2 = d_1 - \sigma\sqrt{T}$$

where

$P_s$ = the current price of the share

$P_x$ = the exercise price of the call

e = 2.7183

RF = the continuously compounded annual risk-free rate

$\sigma$ = the standard deviation of the continuously compounded annual rate of return on share

$I_n$ = the natural log of the bracketed number

T = the time remaining to expiration on an annual basis

$Nd_1$ and $Nd_2$ = the value of the cumulative normal distribution at $d_1$ and $d_2$

**Illustration 7.7:** Calculate a call option price by applying the Black-Scholes options pricing model on the following values:

| | |
|---|---|
| Strike price | = ₹ 45 |
| Time remaining to expiration | = 183 days |
| Current stock price | = ₹ 47 |
| Expected price volatility = Standard Deviation | = 25 |
| Risk-free rate | = 10% |

**Solution:**

Applying the Black-Scholes formula:

$$V_c = P_s\,(Nd_1) - \frac{P}{e\,(RF)\,(T)} \times (Nd_2)$$

$$d_1 = \frac{\ln(47/45) + (0.10 + 0.5)\,(0.25)^2\,(0.5)}{0.25\sqrt{0.5}} = 0.6172$$

$$d_2 = 0.6172 - 0.25/\sqrt{0.5} = 0.4404$$

From a normal distribution table:

N (0.6172) = 0.7315 and

N (0.4404) = 0.6702

$\therefore$ $C = 47\,(0.7315) - 45\,(e^{-(0.10)\,(0.5)})\,(0.6702)$

= ₹ 5.69

**Illustration 7.8:** The data relating to X Ltd. is given below:

| | |
|---|---|
| Current price of share | ₹ 60 |
| Exercise Price | ₹ 56 |

Standard Deviation of continuously compounded:

| | |
|---|---|
| Annual Returns | 0.3 |
| Years to maturity | 0.5 |
| Interest rate per annum | ₹ 14% |

You are required to determine the value of option.

**Solution:**

$$d_1 = \frac{0.0689 + 0.0925}{0.2121} = \frac{0.1615}{0.2121} = 0.7614$$

$d_2 = 0.7614 - 0.2121 = 0.5493$

$N(d_1) = N(0.7614) = 0.7768$

$N(d_1) = N(0.5493) = 0.7086$

$$\text{P.V. of Exercise Price} = \frac{₹\,56}{e^{0.14\times 0.5}} = ₹\,52.21$$

$\therefore$ Co = (₹ 60 × 0.7768) – (₹ 52.21 × 0.7086)

= ₹ 46.61 – ₹ 37.00

= ₹ 9.61.

## 7.8 EXERCISES

1. What is an option?
2. Explain the terms intrinsic value of options and time value of options?
3. What are the factor affecting the value of options?
4. Explain different types of options?
5. Explain the Binomial model for option valuations?
6. Explain Black-Scholes model for option valuation?
7. Write short note on:
   (a) Put Option (b) Call Option
   (c) Striking Price (d) Option Price
   (e) Call Option Boundaries.
8. A stock is currently selling at ₹ 60. The call option on the stock exercisable a year from now at an exercise price of ₹ 55 is currently selling for ₹ 15. The risk-free interest rate is 12%. The stock can either rise or fall after a year. It can fall by 30 per cent. By what price it will rise?
   (Answer: 35%)
9. The data related to Z Ltd. is given below:
   S = 60, u = 1.4, d = 0.8
   E = 50, r = 12, R = 1.12
   What is the value of call option?
   (Answer: ₹ 16.15)
10. Consider the call option on the stock of 'A' Ltd. The stock currently trades for ₹ 22.75. The option has one month to expiration and an exercise price of ₹ 20. The riskless rate is 5% p.a. and the variance of the stock is 0.45.
   (a) What is the value of call option?
   (b) If the risk-free interest rate is 7%, instead of 5%, then what is the value of option?

# Chapter 8 VALUATION IN ACQUISITIONS

8.1 Introduction
8.2 Mergers and Acquisitions
8.3 Reasons for Mergers and Acquisitions
8.4 Procedure for Mergers and Acquisitions
8.5 Determination of Firm's Value
8.6 SEBI Regulations as to Takeovers
8.7 Contents of Scheme of Merger or Acquisition
8.8 Methods of Payment in Merger Transactions
8.9 Illustrations
8.10 Exercises

## 8.1 INTRODUCTION

Corporate restructuring is a broad array of activities which expands or contracts a firm's operations substantially. It brings about a significant change in the organisational structure and internal functioning. The most common forms of corporate restructuring are Mergers and Acquisitions. It also includes activities such as Amalgamation, Takeover, Sale/Purchase of business, Demergers and Performance improvements. Mergers and Acquisition have become a major force in the financial and economic environment, all over the world. It is essentially an American phenomenon. American companies have become a dominant global business since 1970s.

In India, companies have been seriously looking at mergers, acquisition and restructuring, which have became the order of the day. Most of the business groups have been engaged in some kind of corporate restructuring. Therefore, the price and intensity of corporate restructuring has increased, particularly after economic liberalisation. There are greater competitive pressures and more permissive environment. Growth constitutes one of the prime objectives of the business organisations. It can be achieved internally or externally. The growth process can be facilitated externally by acquisition of existing business firms. The acquisition may be in the form of mergers, acquisitions, amalgamation, takeovers, absorptions and consolidations. The finance manager's job is to evaluate such merger/acquisition decision. Those decisions are analogous to capital budgeting decisions. The cost of present investment is to be compared with the expected future benefits, according to the merging firm.

The firm will opt for merger, if it adds to the wealth of the shareholders. Therefore, valuation of Mergers and acquisitions are very important in recent years.

## 8.2 MERGERS AND ACQUISITIONS

The following terms are commonly used in this respect:

(a) **Merger:** When the business of one company is mixed with the other company, it is called merger of companies. In this case, one company goes into liquidation and the other company continues its business. Mergers may be horizontal, vertical and conglomerate. A horizontal merger means, merger of companies engaged in the similar business line. Vertical merger means, a merger of companies engaged in different stages of production in an industry. A conglomerate is a merger of companies engaged in un-related lines of business.

(b) **Acquisition:** Acquisition involves purchase of certain amount of equity capital of a company, in order to exercise control over the affairs of the company. It is also known as take-over. The acquirer should buy at least 50% of the paid up capital of the acquiree company. However, in actual practice, effective control can be exercised with 20 to 40 per cent of Equity Capital, because the remaining shareholders are scattered and they cannot challenge the control of the acquirer company. SEBI has issued guidelines for acquisition or take over of the listed companies. The Acquirer company should buy the shares of acquiree company from the stock market by making an open offer. In case of acquisition, both the companies continue their business. However, there is a change in the management of the acquiree company.

(c) **Absorption:** When one company acquires the business of the other company it is known as absorption. Normally, a loss making company or a weak company sells its business to a financially strong company. The shareholders are issued shares of the acquirer company. In case of absorption, one company goes into liquidation, and the business is absorbed by the other company. It is like a merger.

(d) **Amalgamation:** When two or more companies combine their business, it is called amalgamation. In this case, two or more companies go into liquidation, and a new company is formed to take over the business.

## 8.3 REASONS FOR MERGERS AND ACQUISITIONS

The principal economic rationale of a merger is that, the value of the combined entity is expected to be greater than the sum of the independent values of merging companies. Therefore, the following are the reasons for Mergers and Acquisitions.

1. **Economies of scale:** The operating cost reduction in terms of economies of scale is considered to be the primary motive for mergers and acquisitions.
2. **Synergy:** Synergy is the result of complementary activities. One company may have a substantial amount of financial resources, while the other company may be having profitable investment opportunities. Similarly, one company may have a strong research and development, while the other company may have a very efficiently organised production department.
3. **Fast growth:** Mergers and Acquisitions enable companies to grow faster than the internal expansion route.
4. **Tax benefits:** Tax benefit is another motive for mergers and acquisitions. Tax laws allow set offs and carry forward of losses of companies. Therefore, it is beneficial to merge a company

with a large carry forward losses, with a company having sufficient profits. The merged companies are taxed on the basis of combined profit or losses.

5. **Diversification:** A merger between two unrelated companies would tend to reduce business risk, which in turn reduces the required rate of return of the company's earnings. Thus, it helps to increase the market value of the company.
6. **Strategic benefits:** If a company has decided to expand in a particular industry, acquisition of another company in that industry may offer several strategic benefits. It can prevent a competitor from establishing a similar position in the industry. It is less risky as well as less costly.
7. **Utilisation of surplus:** A company in a matured industry may generate a lot of cash, but may not have opportunities for profitable investment. A merger with another company involving cash compensation also represents a more efficient utilisation of surplus funds.
8. **Managerial efficiency:** A merger may be in the form of greater congruence between the interests of the managers and the shareholders. A merger may result into an increase in managerial effectiveness.

## 8.4 PROCEDURE FOR MERGERS AND ACQUISITIONS

Section 391 to 394 of the Companies Act 1956 provides for Mergers and Acquisitions. Mergers and Acquisitions are complicated transactions involving fairly complex legal, tax and accounting considerations. The following steps should be taken to carry out Mergers and Acquisitions transactions.

1. **Object clause:** The object clause of Memorandum of both the companies should be examined for considering the proposal of Mergers and Acquisitions. If the objects clause permits for such proposals, then the management can go ahead with the proposal. Otherwise the object clause or Articles of the company should be altered, which will be favourable for the purpose of Mergers and Acquisitions.
2. **Approval of the Boards:** The draft proposal for Mergers and Acquisitions should be approved by the respective Board of Directors. The Board should pass a resolution to that effect.
3. **Intimation to Stock Exchange:** The Stock Exchange where the companies are listed should be informed about the proposal of Mergers and Acquisitions.
4. **Shareholders approval:** The proposal of Mergers and Acquisitions should be approved by the shareholders in their meeting. There is a need for passing a special resolution for this purpose.
5. **Approval from respective High courts:** The companies should present a petition to their respective High courts for the confirmation of the scheme. The High court will pass an order, sanctioning the same, after hearing the parties concerned.
6. **Filing the order with the Registrar:** The copies of the High Court order, resolution and proposal should be filed with the Registrar of Companies within the specified time.
7. **Implementation:** All the assets and liabilities of the companies should be transferred as per the scheme, with effect from the appointed date. The payment settlement should be made either in cash or shares, as the case may be. The shares or debentures should be issued as per the terms and conditions stated in the scheme.
8. **Accounting:** The accounting treatment of Mergers and Acquisitions should be given as per the Accounting Standard 14, stated by the Institute of Chartered Accountants of India. The post merger Balance Sheet of the company should be prepared as per the guidelines.

## 8.5 DETERMINATION OF THE FIRM'S VALUE

The problem in the analysis of a potential merger involves determination of the value of the acquiree firm. The value of a firm depends, not only upon its earnings but also upon the operating and financial conditions of the acquiring firm. However, it is not possible to place a single value for the acquiree firm. Thus, a range of value is determined, which are economically justifiable to the prospective acquirers. The final price may be negotiated within this range by the two firms. In order to determine an acceptable price, a number of factors should be considered. The qualitative factors include, managerial talent, strong sales staff and excellent production department. The quantitative factors include, the value of assets and earnings of the company. Thus, the focus of determining the value of a firm is based on several quantitive variables. The following values are also important.

(a) **Book value:** The book value of a firm is based on the balance sheet value of the owner's equity. The net assets are divided by the number of equity shares outstanding for deciding the book value. However, the book value is based on historical costs of the assets of the firm, and therefore has certain limitations.

(b) **Market value:** The market value is the value of shares quoted in the stock market. It is the true worth of a firm, because the market quotations indicate the consensus of investors as to the firm's earning potentials and risk. The market value approach is one of the most widely used method in determining the value of a share of a company. The market value provides a close approximation of the value of a firm. A certain percentage of premium to the market price is often offered, as an inducement for the current owner to sell their shares. However, the market value can change abruptly, as a result of change, not only in analytical factors, but also due to speculative influences. It is also subject to market sentiments and personal decisions.

(c) **Appraisal value:** Appraisal value is the value acquired from an independent appraisal agency. The appraisal value is normally based on the replacement cost. It is an important factor in special situations, where an organisation has been operating at a loss. A company operating at a loss may only be worth its liquidation value. Appraisal by independent appraisers may permit reduction in accounting goodwill by increasing the recognised worth of specific assets. It also provides a test of the reasonableness of the result obtained through the methods based on the going concern concept. The Appraiser also identifies the strengths and weaknesses of the firms. However, this value is not adequate, because the value of the individual assets may have little relation to the firms overall ability to generate earnings. Thus, the appraisal value procedure is useful, if it is carried out in conjunction with other evaluation processes.

(d) **Earnings per share:** The value of a prospective acquisition is considered to be a function of the impact of the merger on the Earning Per Share (EPS). The analysis could focus on, whether the acquisition will have a positive impact on the EPS after the merger, or whether it will have the effect of diluting the EPS. The future EPS will affect the firms share price, because of the function of Price/Earning Ratio.

## 8.6 SEBI REGULATIONS AS TO TAKEOVERS

The Securities and Exchange Board of India has framed the regulations for hostile takeovers and bailout takeovers. These regulations are as follows:

1. Any Acquirer who acquires shares or voting rights of more than 5, 10 or 14 per cent in a listed company, shall disclose at every stage, the aggregate of the shareholding or voting rights to the concerned target company and stock exchanges, where the shares are listed.
2. The Acquirer shall also disclose the purchase or sale aggregating 2% or more of the share capital of the target company, within 2 days to the company and the concerned stock exchanges, in which the company's shares are listed.
3. The Acquirer, who holds more than 15 per cent share or voting rights in any company, shall, within 21 days from the financial year ending March 31, make disclosure on yearly basis.
4. A promoter or every person having control over the company, shall disclose to the company, the number and percentage of shares or voting rights held by him and by the persons acting in concert, shall inform within 21 days of the end of the financial year on 31st March, and record date of the company for the purpose of declaration of dividend.
5. Any Acquirer can acquire 15 per cent or more of shares or voting rights in a company, individually or acting in concert, by making a public announcement to acquire shares of such company, in accordance with the regulations.
6. Any additional acquisitions of shares or voting rights entitling him to exercise more than 5 per cent of voting rights in any financial year ending on 31st March, unless such acquirer makes a public announcement to acquire the shares. This provision entails him to acquire 15% or more, but less than 75% of the shares or voting rights in a company.
7. An acquirer, irrespective of his shareholding in the company shall not have control over the target company, unless he makes a public announcement to acquire the shares in accordance with these regulations.
8. The public offer shall be, as per the provisions contained in the SEBI Regulations, 1997.
9. These provisions shall not apply to any change in control, which takes place in pursuance of a special resolution, passed by the shareholders in a general meeting.
10. The person acquiring shares from the promoters or financial institutions, shall make a public announcement of his intention to acquire shares from other shareholders of the company.

## 8.7 CONTENTS OF SCHEME OF MERGERS AND ACQUISITIONS

The contents of any model scheme of Mergers, Amalgamation or Acquisition will be as follows:

1. **Transfer date**: It is usually the first day of the financial year, for which the audited accounts are available with the companies. It is a cut-off date, from which all the movable and immovable properties shall be transferred.
2. **Effective date:** It is the date on which the transfer and vesting of the undertaking of Transferor Company shall take effect.
3. **Arrangement:** The arrangement should be entered into with the secured and unsecured creditors, including Debenture-holders.
4. **Exchange ratio:** It is the ratio of exchange of shares of the companies, which is worked out, based on the valuation of shares of the respective companies, as per the audited accounts, accepted methods and valuation guidelines.
5. **Reduction of share capital:** It is necessary, when the shares of one company are held by the other company or subsidiaries.
6. **Pending Receipt of the Requisite Approvals:** Before the receipt of necessary approvals to the merger or amalgamation, the transferor company possesses the property to be transferred and to carry out the business for and on behalf of and in trust for the Transferee Company.

7. **Terms of scheme:** The terms of scheme may be suitably provided, for the transfer of the whole or part of the undertaking, property or liabilities of transferor company to the transferee company, dissolution of the firm, employees of the transferee company, distending shareholders, creditors and other agencies.

## 8.8 METHODS OF PAYMENT

The following methods of payment are used in case of Mergers and Acquisitions:

(a) **Cash:** The shareholders of the Acquiree Company are paid cash by the Acquirer Company. This is usually followed, in case of Acquisition by public offer to buy shares from the stock market.

(b) **Shares:** A share for share exchange is often used as a method of payment in combinations involving large companies.

(c) **Loan stock:** The Acquirer company issues loan stock, i.e., debentures to the shareholders of Acquiree Company. In this method an equity investment is exchanged with a fixed interest investment.

(d) **Convertible debentures:** The shareholders of Acquiree Company are issued convertible debentures of Acquirer Company. Thus, the shares of one company are exchanged with convertible debentures of the other company. The shareholders get the fixed interest security, which is convertible into an equity investment at some time in the future. If the future price moves in his favour, he will be able to take up his equity interest.

## 8.9 ILLUSTRATIONS

**Illustration 8.1:** The following are the balance sheet of Jay Ltd. and Vijay Ltd. as on 31st March, 2012:

| Particulars | Jay Ltd. (₹ lakhs) | Vijay Ltd. (₹ lakhs) |
|---|---|---|
| **Liabilities:** | | |
| Equity Shares Capital (₹ 10 each) | 40 | 18 |
| General Reserve | 50 | 10 |
| Profit & loss account | 30 | 08 |
| 12% Debentures | 35 | – |
| Creditors | 20 | 10 |
| Bills Payables | 05 | 04 |
| **Total** | **180** | **50** |
| **Assets:** | | |
| Fixed Assets | 70 | 30 |
| Investments | 50 | – |
| Current Assets | 60 | 20 |
| **Total** | **180** | **50** |

The Board of directors of Jay Ltd. approved a take over of Vijay Ltd. as on 30th June, 2012. You are required to find out the ratio of exchange of shares on the basis of Book value.

**Solution:**

(a) Calculation of Intrinsic value of shares

| Particulars | Jay Ltd. (₹ lakhs) | Vijay Ltd. (₹ lakhs) |
|---|---|---|
| Fixed Assets | 70 | 30 |
| Investments | 50 | – |
| Current Assets | 60 | 20 |
| **Total Assets** | **180** | **50** |
| *Less*: **Liabilities** | | |
| Creditors | 20 | 10 |
| Bills Payables | 05 | 04 |
| 12% Debentures | 35 | – |
| **Total Liabilities** | **60** | **14** |
| **Net assets** | 120 | 36 |
| Number of equity shares in lakhs | 4 | 1.80 |
| ∴ Intrinsic value per share (Book value) | 30 | 20 |

(b) Calculation of ratio of exchange

Value of shares of Jay Ltd. ₹ 30. Value of share of Vijay Ltd. ₹ 20. Thus, the ratio exchange of share on the basis of Book value shall be:

2 Share of Jay Ltd. = 3 shares of Vijay Ltd.

$2 \times 30 =$ ₹ 60 (Jay Ltd.)

$3 \times 20 =$ ₹ 60 (Vijay Ltd.)

Thus, the exchange ratio of shares shall be 2 shares of Jay Ltd. for every 3 shares of Vijay Ltd.

**Illustrations 8.2:** Ajay Ltd. is willing to acquire Vijay Ltd. and the following information is available in respect of these companies:

| Particulars | Ajay Ltd. | Vijay Ltd. |
|---|---|---|
| Number of Equity Shares | 50 lakhs | 30 lakhs |
| Earnings after tax (₹) | 250 lakhs | 90 lakhs |
| Market price per share (₹) | 210 | 140 |

Required:

(a) What is the present EPS of each company?

(b) If the proposed merger takes place, what would be the new EPS for Ajay Ltd., if the exchange ratio is based on market price?

(c) What should be the exchange ratio, if the shareholders of Ajay Ltd. want to ensure the same EPS as before merger?

**Solution:**

(a) $\text{Earning Per Share} = \dfrac{\text{PAT}}{\text{No. of Eq. Shares}}$

$\therefore \text{Ajay Ltd.} = \dfrac{250}{50} = ₹\,5$

$\text{Vijay Ltd.} = \dfrac{90}{30} = ₹\,3$

(b) Calculation of EPS after merger

The exchange ratio is based on market price

∴ Exchange Ratio = 140:210

= 2:3

2 shares of Ajay Ltd. for every 3 shares of Vijay Ltd.

$\therefore 210 \times 2 = 420$

$\therefore 140 \times 3 = 420$

∴ No of shares to be issued to Vijay Ltd. = $\dfrac{2}{3} \times 30 \text{ lakhs} = 20 \text{ lakh shares}$.

∴ Total Shares with Ajay Ltd.

50 lakhs + 20 lakhs = 70 lakhs

Total earnings after Tax = 250 + 90 = ₹ 340 lakhs.

$\therefore \text{EPS after Merger} = \dfrac{\text{PAT}}{\text{No. of Equity Shares}}$

$= \dfrac{340}{70} = ₹\,4.86$

(c) Calculation of new exchange ratio

The number of shares to be exchanged by Ajay Ltd. with Vijay Ltd., based on EPS of the respective companies

$= \dfrac{₹\,3}{₹\,5} \times 30 \text{ lakhs} = ₹\,18 \text{ lakhs}$

The number of shares with Ajay Ltd.

= 50 lakhs + 18 lakhs

= 68 lakhs

$\text{EPS after Merger} = \dfrac{340}{68} = ₹\,5$.

∴ The new exchange ratio = 3:5

∴ 3 shares of Ajay Ltd. for every five shares of Vijay Ltd.

**Illustration 8.3:** Red Ltd. is considering the proposal to acquire Yes Ltd. Their financial data is given below:

| Particulars | Red Ltd. | Yes Ltd. |
|---|---|---|
| No. of Equity Shares | 10 lakhs | 6 lakhs |
| Market price per share (₹) | 300 | 180 |
| Market capitalisation (₹) | 3,000 lakhs | 1,080 lakhs |

Red Ltd. intends to pay ₹ 1,400 lakhs in cash for Yes Ltd., if Yes Ltd's market price reflects only its value as a separate entity. You are required to calculate the cost of merger (a) when merger is financed by cash (b) when merger is financed by stock.

**Solution:**

(a) Cost of merger financed by cash

$$\text{Cash} = (\text{Cash} - MV_Y) + (MV_Y - PV_Y)$$

where

$MV_Y$ = Market value of Yes Ltd.

$PV_Y$ = Intrinsic value of Yes Ltd.

$$\therefore \text{Cash} = (1{,}400 - 1{,}080) + (1{,}080 - 1{,}080)$$
$$= ₹\ 320 \text{ lakhs.}$$

(b) Cost of merger when merger is financed by stock

$$\text{Cost of merger} = \propto PV_{RY} - PV_Y$$

where

$PV_{RY}$ = value in Red Ltd. that Yes Ltd. shareholders get,

$\propto$ = proportion

Assume that Red Ltd. agrees to exchange 5 lakh Equity shares in exchange of shares in Yes Ltd., instead of payment in cash of ₹ 1,400 lakhs. Then the cost of merger will be calculated as follows.

$$\text{Cost of merger} = ₹\ (5 \text{ lakhs} \times 300) - 1{,}080 \text{ lakhs}$$
$$= ₹\ 1{,}500 - 1{,}080$$
$$= ₹\ 420 \text{ lakhs.}$$
$$PV_{RY} = PV_R + PV_Y = 3{,}000 + 1{,}080 \text{ lakhs}$$
$$= ₹\ 4{,}080 \text{ lakhs.}$$

∴ Proportion of Yes Ltd's shareholders get in Red Ltd's capital structure

$$= \frac{5 \text{ lakhs}}{10 + 5 \text{ lakhs}} = \frac{5}{15} = 0.33.$$

$$\therefore \text{Cost of merger} = \propto PV_R - PV_Y$$
$$= (0.33 \times 4{,}080) - 1{,}080$$
$$= 1360 - 1080$$
$$= ₹\ 280 \text{ lakhs.}$$

**Illustration 8.4:** Hope Ltd. wants to acquire Weak Ltd. The Balance sheet of Weak Ltd. as on 31[st] March, 2012 was as follows:

| Liabilities | (₹ lakhs) | Assets | (₹ lakhs) |
|---|---|---|---|
| Equity Shares Capital | 400 | Plant & Machinery | 650 |
| (40 lakh Shares) | | Inventory | 135 |
| Retained Earnings | 100 | Debtors | 65 |
| 10.5% Debentures | 200 | Cash & Bank | 10 |
| Creditors | 160 | | |
| | **860** | | **860** |

**Additional Information:**

(i) The shareholders of Weak Ltd. will get 1.5 shares in Hope Ltd. for every 2 shares held. The shares of Hope Ltd. will be issued at its current market price of ₹ 18 per share. The Debentures holders will get 11% Debentures of the equal amount. The external liabilities are expected to be settled at ₹ 150 lakhs.

(ii) The following are projected incremental cash flows expected from acquisition for 6 years.

| Year End | ₹ lakhs |
|---|---|
| 1 | 150 |
| 2 | 200 |
| 3 | 260 |
| 4 | 300 |
| 5 | 220 |
| 6 | 120 |

(iii) The free cash flow of Weak Ltd. is expected to grow at 3 per cent per annum, after 6 years.

(iv) The cost of capital relevant for Weak Ltd.'s cash flow has been determined at 13 per cent.

(v) The acquisition expenses of ₹ 15 lakhs are to be met by the acquiring company.

Required : Determine-

(a) Cost of Acquisition

(b) Financial feasibility of the acquisition.

**Solution:**

(a) Calculation of Cost of Acquisition

| Particulars | (₹ lakhs) |
|---|---|
| 30,00,000 shares $(40 \times \frac{1.5}{2})$ @₹18 | 540 |
| 11% Debentures | 200 |
| Settlement of External Liabilities | 150 |
| Acquisition Expenses | 15 |
| Total | **905** |

(b) Calculation of present value of free cash flow

| Year End | FCFF (₹ lakhs) | P.V. Factory @13% | Total PV (₹ lakhs) |
|---|---|---|---|
| 1 | 150 | 0.885 | 132.75 |
| 2 | 200 | 0.783 | 156.60 |
| 3 | 260 | 0.693 | 180.18 |
| 4 | 300 | 0.613 | 183.90 |
| 5 | 220 | 0.543 | 119.46 |
| 6 | 120 | 0.480 | 57.60 |
| | | | **830.49** |

Present value after the forecast period (C.V.)

$$\text{Continuing Value (CV)} = \frac{\text{FCFF}(1+g)}{k-g}$$

$$= \frac{120\,(1.03)}{0.13-0.03} = \frac{123.60}{0.10} = ₹\,1{,}236 \text{ lakhs}$$

$$\text{Present Value} = ₹\,1{,}236 \times 0.480 \text{ lakhs}$$

$$= ₹\,593.28 \text{ lakhs}$$

Calculation of Net Present Value

| | |
|---|---|
| Present value of Free Cash Flows | ₹ 830.49 lakhs |
| + Present value of Free Cash Flows after the forecast period | 593.28 |
| **Total Present Value** | **1,423.77** |
| Less Cost of Acquisition | 905.00 |
| **Net Present Value** | **518.77** |

As the present value of future cash flows is positive, i.e., ₹ 518.77 lakhs, the Acquisition is feasible.

**Illustration 8.5:** Big Ltd. wants to acquire Small Ltd. by exchanging its 1.6 shares for every share of Small Ltd. It anticipates to maintain the existing P/E Ratio subsequent to the merger. The relevant financial data is as follows:

| **Particulars** | **Big Ltd.** | **Small Ltd.** |
|---|---|---|
| Profit after tax (₹) | 150 lakhs | 45 lakhs |
| Number of Equity Shares | 30 lakhs | 7.5 lakhs |
| Market price per share (₹) | 35 | 40 |

Required:

(i) What is the exchange ratio based on market prices?

(ii) What is the Pre-merger EPS and P/E ratio of each company?

(iii) What is the P/E Ratio used in acquiring Small Ltd?

(iv) What is the EPS of Big Ltd. after acquisition?

(v) What is the expected market price per share of the merged company?

**Solution:**

(i) Exchange ratio based on market prices

$$=\frac{1.6\times 35}{40}=1.4:1$$

(ii) Pre merger EPS and P/E Ratios

| Particulars | Big Ltd. | Small Ltd. |
|---|---|---|
| PAT (₹ lakhs) | 150 | 45 |
| No of shares (lakhs) | 30 | 7.5 |
| $\therefore$ EPS $=\frac{\text{PAT}}{\text{No. of Shares}}$ | $\frac{150}{30}$ = ₹ 5 | $\frac{45}{7.5}$ = ₹ 6 |
| $\therefore$ P/E Ratio $=\frac{\text{MP}}{\text{EPS}}$ | $\frac{35}{5}$ = 7 times | $\frac{40}{6}$ = 6.67 times |

(iii) Calculation of implied P/E Ratio in Acquisition

$$=\frac{\text{Market price of shares offered}}{\text{Current EPS of Big Ltd.}}$$

$$=\frac{₹\ 35\times 1.6}{6}$$

$$=\frac{₹\ 56}{6}=9.3\text{ Times.}$$

(iv) EPS of Merged Company

$$=\frac{\text{PAT of both the Co's}}{\text{Shares of Big Ltd after Merger}}$$

$$=\frac{150+45}{30+12}$$

$$=\frac{195}{42}=₹\ 4.64$$

Number of shares issued to Small Ltd.

= 1.6 × 7.5 = 12 lakhs.

(v) Expected Market price after Merger

EPS after Merger × Pre-merger P/E Ratio of Big Ltd.

= ₹ 4.64 × 7

= ₹ 32.48

**Note:** Big Ltd. expects to maintain P/E ratio of 7, even after merger.

**Illustration 8.6:** Bharat Ltd. is intending to acquire Bhushan Ltd. by merger, and the following information is available in respect of the companies.

| Particulars | Bharat Ltd. | Bhushan Ltd. |
|---|---|---|
| Profit after tax (₹) | 50,00,000 | 18,00,000 |
| Number of Equity Shares | 10,00,000 | 6,00,000 |
| Market price per share (₹) | 42 | 28 |

Required:

(a) What is the present EPS of the companies?

(b) If the proposed merger takes place, what would be the new EPS of Bharat Ltd?

(c) What should be the exchange ratio, if Bhushan Ltd. wants to ensure, the earnings to members are as before the merger took place?

**Solution:**

(a) Present EPS of both the companies

| Particulars | Bharat Ltd. | Bhushan Ltd. |
|---|---|---|
| $EPS = \frac{PAT}{\text{No. of Eq. Shares}}$ | $\frac{50,00,000}{10,00,000}$ = ₹ 5 | $\frac{18,00,000}{6,00,000}$ = ₹ 3 |

(b) Calculation of new EPS after Merger

Number of Equity shares of Bharat Ltd. to be exchanged for Bhushan Ltd., based on market value per share

$$= 6,00,000 \times \frac{28}{42} = 4,00,000 \text{ Shares}$$

∴ Total Equity shares of Bharat Ltd.

$$= 10,00,000 + 4,00,000 = 14,00,000 \text{ Shares.}$$

∴ EPS of Bharat Ltd. after Merger

$$= \frac{PAT}{\text{No. of Equity Shares}} = \frac{50,00,000 + 18,00,000}{10,00,000 + 4,00,000}$$

$$= \frac{68,00,000}{14,00,000} = ₹\ 4.86.$$

(c) Calculation of Exchange ratio, in order to ensure same EPS

No of shares to be exchanged on EPS basis

$$= 6,00,000 \times \frac{3}{5} = 3,60,000 \text{ Shares}$$

∴ Total Equity Shares after Merger

$$= 10,00,000 + 3,60,000$$

$$= 13,60,000 \text{ shares}$$

$$\therefore \text{EPS after Merger} = \frac{68,00,000}{13,60,000}$$

$$= ₹ 5$$

$\therefore$ Exchange Ratio = 3:5

**Illustration 8.7:** The following information is provided related to the acquiring firm Das Ltd. and the target firm Vyas Ltd.

| Particulars | Das Ltd. | Vyas Ltd. |
|---|---|---|
| Profit after tax | ₹ 200 lakhs | ₹ 40 lakhs |
| No of shares outstanding | 20 lakhs | 10 lakhs |
| Price – Earning ratio | 10 | 5 |

Required:

(i) What is the swap ratio based on current market price?

(ii) What is the EPS of Das Ltd. after acquisition?

(iii) What is the expected market price per share of Das Ltd. after acquisition, assuming P/E Ratio remains unchanged?

(iv) Determine the market value of merged firm.

(v) Calculate gain/loss for shareholders of the two independent companies after acquisition.

**Solution:**

(i) EPS before Acquisition

Das Ltd. = 200 ÷ 20 = ₹ 10

Vyas Ltd. = 40 ÷ 10 = ₹ 4

$\therefore$ Market price of share before acquisition

= P/E Ratio × EPS

$\therefore$ Das Ltd. = 10 × 10 = ₹ 100

Vyas Ltd. = 4 × 5= ₹ 20

$$\therefore \text{Swap Ratio} = \frac{20}{100} = 0.2 \text{ or } 1:5$$

One share of Das Ltd. for every five shares of Vyas Ltd.

$\therefore$ Number of shares to be issued

= 10 × 0.2 = 2 lakhs.

(ii) EPS after Acquisition

$$= \frac{\text{PAT}}{\text{No. of Shares}} = \frac{200+40}{20+2} = \frac{240}{22} = ₹10.91$$

(iii) Expected market price per share of Das Ltd. after acquisition

Market price = P/E Ratio × EPS

= 10 × 10.91

= ₹ 109.10

(iv) Market value of Merged Firm

= No of Shares × Market Price per Share

= ₹ (22 lakhs × 109.10)

= ₹ 2,400 lakhs.

(v) Gain from the merger

| Particulars | (₹ lakhs) |
|---|---|
| Post Merger Market Value | 2,400 |
| *Less*: Pre Merger Market Value | |
| Das 20 × 100 | 2,000 |
| Vyas 10 × 20 | 200 |
| Gain from the merger | **200** |

**Gain to the shareholders**

| Particulars | Das Ltd. | Vyas Ltd. |
|---|---|---|
| Post merger value | 2,182 | 218 |
| *Less*: Pre merger value | 2,000 | 200 |
| Gain | **182** | **18** |

**Illustration 8.8:** A Ltd. is considering take over of B Ltd. and C Ltd. The financial data for the three companies is given below:

| Particulars | A Ltd. | B Ltd. | C Ltd. |
|---|---|---|---|
| Equity share capital (₹ 10 each) | ₹ 450 lakhs | 180 lakhs | 90 lakhs |
| Profit after Tax | ₹ 90 lakhs | 18 lakhs | 18 lakhs |
| Market Price (₹) | 60 | 35 | 45 |

Required:

(i) Calculate the P/E Ratio

(ii) Calculate EPS of A Ltd. after take over of B Ltd. and C Ltd. separately. Which take over will you recommend?

**Solution:**

(i) Calculation of P/E Ratio

| Particulars | A Ltd. | B Ltd. | C Ltd. |
|---|---|---|---|
| Profit after tax (₹ lakhs) | 90 | 18 | 18 |
| No of shares (lakhs) | 45 | 18 | 9 |
| EPS | 2 | 1 | 2 |
| Market Price (₹) | 60 | 35 | 45 |
| ∴ P/E Ratio | 60 ÷ 2 | 35 ÷ 1 | 45 ÷ 2 |
| | 30 | 35 | 22.5 |

(ii) Calculation of EPS after acquisition

$$\text{Exchange Ratio} = \frac{\text{Buyer's P/E Ratio}}{\text{Seller's P/E Ratio}}$$

$$\text{For B Ltd.} = \frac{30}{35} = 0.81$$

$$\text{For C Ltd.} = \frac{30}{22.5} = 1.30$$

| Particulars | A Ltd. | B Ltd. | C Ltd. |
|---|---|---|---|
| Exchange Ratio | – | 0.81 | 1.30 |
| Value of Shares (₹ lakhs) (M.P. × No. of Shares) | 2,700 | 630 | 405 |
| No. of A Ltd's shares to be given | | 630/60 | 405/60 |
| | | 10.5 lakhs | 6.75 lakhs |
| Total Earnings after Acquisition (₹ lakhs) | | 108 | 108 |
| Total No of Shares after Acquisition (lakhs) | | 55.5 | 51.75 |
| EPS after acquisition (₹) | | 1.95 | 2.08 |

Takeover of 'C' Ltd. by 'A' Ltd. gives higher E.P.S. i.e. ₹ 2.08. Hence, takeover of 'C' Ltd. is recommended in order to increase the value to the shareholders of 'A' Ltd.

**Illustration 8.9:** X Ltd. is contemplating the purchase of Y Ltd. X Ltd. has 3 lakh shares having a market price of ₹ 30 each. Y Ltd. has 2 lakh shares selling at ₹ 20 per share. The EPS of X Ltd. is ₹ 4, while that of Y Ltd. is ₹ 2.25. The management of both the companies are negotiating two alternative proposals for exchange of shares. The first alternative is to exchange the shares in proportion to relative earnings per share. The other alternative is to issue 0.5 shares of 'X' Ltd. for every share of 'Y' Ltd.

You are required to:

(a) Calculate the Earnings Per Share after merger of the two alternatives

(b) Show the impact on EPS for the shareholders of two companies under both the alternatives.

**Solution:**

(a) (i) Calculation of total earnings after merger

| Particulars | X Ltd. | Y Ltd. | Total |
|---|---|---|---|
| Outstanding shares | 3,00,000 | 2,00,000 | – |
| EPS (₹) | 4 | 2.25 | – |
| Total Earnings (₹) | 12,00,000 | 4,50,000 | 16,50,000 |

(ii) Calculation of number of shares after merger

| | |
|---|---|
| X Ltd. | 3,00,000 |
| Y Ltd. $2{,}00{,}000 \times \frac{2.25}{4}$ | 1,12,500 |
| Total | **4,12,500** |

$$\therefore \text{ EPS after Merger} = \frac{\text{Total Profit}}{\text{Total Shares}}$$

$$= \frac{16,50,000}{4,12,500} = ₹\,4$$

(iii) Calculation of EPS when exchanges ratio is 0.5:1

Total Earnings = ₹ 12,00,000 + 4,50,000 = 16,50,000

Total number of shares =

| | |
|---|---|
| X Ltd. | 3,00,000 |
| Y Ltd. (2,00,000 × 0.5) | 1,00,000 |
| Total | **4,00,000** |

(iv) EPS after merger = $\frac{16,50,000}{4,00,000} = ₹\,4.125.$

(b) Impact of merger on EPS

(i) Impact on shareholders of 'X' Ltd.

| | |
|---|---|
| EPS before merger | ₹ 4.00 |
| EPS after merger | ₹ 4.125 |
| Increase in EPS | **0.125** |

$$\therefore \%\text{ Increase} = \frac{0.125}{4} \times 100 = 3.1\%.$$

(ii) Impact on shareholders of 'Y' Ltd.

| | ₹ |
|---|---|
| Equivalent EPS before merger (2.25/0.5) | 4.500 |
| EPS after merger | 4.125 |
| Decrease in EPS | **0.375** |

$$\therefore \%\text{ Decrease} = \frac{0.375}{4.500} \times 100 = 8.3\%.$$

**Illustration 8.10:** Following are the financial statements of 'A' Ltd. and 'B' Ltd. for the financial year ended 31st March, 2012. Both the companies operate in the same industry.

| **Balance Sheet** | **(₹ lakhs)** | |
|---|---|---|
| **Particulars** | **A Ltd.** | **B Ltd.** |
| Fixed Assets | 10 | 5 |
| Current Assets | 14 | 10 |
| Total | **24** | **15** |
| Equity Share Capital | 10 | 8 |
| Reserves and Surplus | 2 | – |
| Debentures | 5 | 3 |
| Current Liabilities | 7 | 4 |
| Total | **24** | **15** |

| **Income Statement** | (₹ lakhs) | |
|---|---|---|
| | **A Ltd.** | **B Ltd.** |
| Net Sales | 34.50 | 17.00 |
| Cost of goods sold | 27.60 | 13.60 |
| Gross profit | 6.90 | 3.40 |
| Operating expenses | 2.00 | 1.00 |
| Interest | 0.70 | 0.42 |
| EBIT | 4.20 | 1.98 |
| Taxes @30% | 1.26 | 0.59 |
| Profit after tax | 2.94 | 1.39 |

**Additional information:**

| | | |
|---|---|---|
| Number of Equity shares | 1,00,000 | 80,000 |
| Dividend payout ratio | 40% | 60% |
| Market Price per share (₹) | 40 | 15 |

Assume that the two firms are in the process of negotiating a merger through an exchange of equity shares.

You are required to:

(a) Determine the share prices of both the companies into EPS and P/E components.

(b) Estimate future EPS growth rates of each firm.

(c) Determine the upper and lower limits of exchange ratios.

(d) Calculate the post-merger EPS based on an exchange ratio of 0.4:1 being offered by A Ltd.

(e) Estimate the post merger market prices.

**Solution:**

(a) Determination of EPS and P/E Ratios

| **Particulars** | **A Ltd.** | **B Ltd.** |
|---|---|---|
| Profit after tax (₹ lakhs) | 2.94 | 1.39 |
| Number of shares | 1,00,000 | 80,000 |
| ∴ EPS (₹) | 2.94 | 1.74 |
| Market Price (₹) | 40 | 15 |
| ∴ P/E Ratio | 13.6 Times | 8.62 Times |

(b) Estimate of growth rates in EPS

Retention Ratio = 60%, 40%

$$\therefore \text{Return on Equity} = \frac{\text{PAT}}{\text{Equity \& Res}} \times 100$$

$$\text{A Ltd.} = \frac{2.94}{12} \times 100 = 24.5\%$$

$$\text{B Ltd.} = \frac{1.39}{8} \times 100 = 17.375\%$$

$$\text{Growth Rate} = \text{ROE} \times \text{Retention Ratio}$$

$$\text{A Ltd.} = 24.5\% \times 60\%$$

$$= 14.7\%$$

$$\text{B Ltd.} = 17.375 \times 40\%$$

$$= 6.95\%$$

(c) Equity Share Exchange Ratio

(i) Market Price Based $= \dfrac{\text{MPSB}}{\text{MPSA}} = \dfrac{₹\,15}{40} = 0.375 : 1$

(ii) Book value Based

$$\text{Book value} = \frac{\text{Eq + Res}}{\text{No. of Eq. Shares}}$$

$$\text{A Ltd.} = \frac{12{,}00{,}000}{1{,}00{,}000} = ₹\,12$$

$$\text{B Ltd.} = \frac{8{,}00{,}000}{80{,}000} = ₹\,10$$

$$\therefore \text{Exchange Ratio} = \frac{\text{BVB}}{\text{BVA}} = \frac{10}{12} = 0.83:1$$

$\therefore$ Lower limit exchange ratio = 0.375:1

$\therefore$ Upper limit exchange ratio = 0.83:1

(d) Calculation of post merger EPS based on exchange ratio of 0.4:1

Total profit = 2.94 + 1.39 = ₹ 4.33 lakhs

Shares outstanding

A Ltd. + B Ltd. = 1,00,000 + 32,000

= 1,32,000

$$\therefore \text{EPS} = \frac{4{,}33{,}000}{1{,}32{,}000} = ₹\,3.28.$$

(e) Estimate of Post-Merger Market Prices

| Particulars | A Ltd. | B Ltd. | Combined |
|---|---|---|---|
| EPS | 2.94 | 1.74 | 4.68 |
| P/E Ratio | 13.6 | 8.62 | 13.6 |
| Market Price | 40 | 15 | 63.65 |
| MPS dilution | 23.65 | 10.2 | |

| | |
|---|---|
| MPS claim per old share = 63 × 0.4 = | ₹ 25.2 |
| *Less*: MPS per old share = | ₹ 15.0 |
| | 10.2 |

## 8.10 EXERCISES

1. What is a Merger? How does it differ from Acquisition?
2. Explain the legal procedure for Mergers and Acquisitions.
3. What are the reasons for Mergers and Acquisitions?
4. Explain the SEBI regulations for Takeovers.
5. Explain the important contents of the scheme of Merger and Acquisition.
6. What are the methods of payment in Mergers and Acquisitions?
7. Write short note on:
   (a) Merger (b) Acquisition
   (c) Amalgamation (d) Strategic Benefit
   (e) Demerger.
8. 'A' Ltd. wants to acquire 'B' Ltd. The exchange ratio is fixed at 0.5:1. The relevant financial data is as follows:

| Particulars | A Ltd. | B Ltd. |
|---|---|---|
| Profit after tax | ₹ 18 lakhs | 3.6 lakhs |
| Equity shares outstanding | 6 lakhs | 1.8 lakhs |
| Earnings per share (₹) | 3 | 2 |
| P/E Ratio | 10 | 7 |
| Market price per share (₹) | 30 | 14 |

Required:

1. What is the number of equity shares required to be issued by A Ltd?
2. What would the EPS of A Ltd. after acquisition?
3. What would be the expected market price per share of A Ltd?
4. Determine the market value of the merged firm.

(Answer: 90,000, ₹ 3.13, ₹ 31.30, ₹ 215.97 lakhs)

9. Young Ltd. is studying the possible acquisition of Old Ltd. by way of merger. The following data is available in respect of the companies:

| Particulars | Young Ltd. | Old Ltd. |
|---|---|---|
| Profit after tax (₹) | 20,00,000 | 6,00,000 |
| Number of equity shares | 4,00,000 | 1,00,000 |
| Market price per share (₹) | 150 | 120 |

Required:

(a) If the merger goes through by exchange of equity shares and the exchange ratio is based on the current market price, what is the new earnings per share for Young Ltd?

(b) Old Ltd. wants to be sure that the earnings available to its shareholders will not be reduced by the merger? What should be the exchange ratio in that case?

(Answer: (a) ₹ 5.42, (b) 1.20:1)

10. Strong Ltd. wants to acquire Weak Ltd. The Balance sheet of Weak Ltd. as on 31st March, 2012 was as follows:

| Liabilities | ₹ | Assets | ₹ |
|---|---|---|---|
| Equity share capital (₹ 10 each) | 6,00,000 | Machinery | 11,00,000 |
| Reserve & Surplus | 2,00,000 | Stock | 1,70,000 |
| 12% Debentures | 2,00,000 | Debtors | 30,000 |
| Creditors | 3,20,000 | Cash | 20,000 |
| | **13,20,000** | | **13,20,000** |

**Additional Information:**

(i) The shareholders of Weak Ltd. will get one share in Strong Ltd. for every two shares. External liabilities were to be settled at ₹ 3,00,000. The shares would be issued at its current price of ₹ 15 each. Debenture holders will get 13% convertible debentures in Strong Ltd. for the same amount. Debtors and inventories are expected to realise ₹ 1,80,000.

(ii) Strong Ltd. has decided to operate the business of Weak Ltd. as a separate division. The division is likely to give cash flows after tax to the extent of ₹ 3,00,000 per year for the next 6 years. Strong Ltd. has planned that after 6 years, the division would be demerged and disposed off for ₹ 1,00,000.

(iii) The company's cost of capital is 14%.

You are required to advise whether the Acquisition is feasible?

(P.V. of ₹ 1 for six years @14% = 0.8772, 0.7695, 0.6750, 0.5921, 0.5194 and 0.4556)

(Answer: NPV is positive hence Acquisition is feasible)

# Chapter 9 VALUE ENHANCEMENT

9.1 Introduction
9.2 Value Enhancement
9.3 Discounted Cash Flow
9.4 Economic Value Added
9.5 Free Cash Flow
9.6 Return on Investment
9.7 Exercises

## 9.1 INTRODUCTION

A business proposal raises value of the firm only if the present value of the future streams of cash benefits expected from the proposal is higher than the initial cash outlay required to implement the proposal. This is the fundamental principle of finance. Financial decisions involve alternative courses of action. These alternatives have different risk-return implications. The prime goal for any company is to maximise the market value of equity shares of the company. The market price of a share is an index of the performance of the company. It also takes into account the present and prospective future earnings per share, risk associated with the business, dividend and retention policies of the company. The share of a company is a movable property and it can be transferred from person to person.

The value of company indicates the net assets as shown in the books of accounts. Thus, the value of a company's business is based on the net assets. It is the simplest form of valuation of business enterprise. The net asset valuation is the difference between the assets and liabilities based on the balance sheet values. The capital structure of a company may include both debt as well as equity. The financial statements contain a wealth of information. The analysis and interpretation of the financial statements provides valuable insights into the company's performance and financial position. The balance sheet shows the financial status of a business at a given date. The profit and loss account is the summary of revenues and expenses and the difference between the two is either profit or loss.

## 9.2 VALUE ENHANCEMENT

The primary objective of a company is to earn profit. Therefore, the objective of financial management is also profit maximization. It implies that the finance manager has to take decisions in a manner so that the profits of a company are maximized. However, profit maximization cannot be the sole objective of a company. Profit maximization has to be attempted with a realisation of risk involved. There is a direct relationship between risk and profit. The shareholder value maximization model holds that the primary goal of the firm is to maximize the market value of the company.

Value of a company is represented by the market price of the company's shares. The market price of a company's share represents the focal judgment of all stockholders. It takes into account present and prospective future earnings per share, the timing and risk of these earnings, the dividend policy of the company and many other factors that bear upon the market price of the share. The market price serves as a performance index of the firms progress. It indicates how well management is doing on behalf of stockholders.

Stakeholders hire managers to run their company for them because they have absolute power to hire. Managers set aside their interest and maximize stock price because markets are efficient. Stakeholders wealth is maximized because lenders are fully protected from shareholders actions. Firm value is maximized because there are no costs created for society. In any company, the management is the decision making authority. As a tendency the management may pursue its goal of profit maximization. But in an organisation where there is significant outside participation the management may not be able to exclusively pursue its personal goals due to the constant supervision of the various stakeholders of the company, i.e., employees, creditor, customers and government. The wealth maximization objective is generally in accordance with the interests of the various groups such as owners, employees, creditors and society.

The net present worth of a company can be determined as follows:

$$V = G - C$$

where

V = Value of a company

G = Gross net worth

C = Investment of equity capital

Alternatively the value of a company can also be determined as follows:

$$V = \frac{E}{K}$$

where

V = Value of company

E = Future earnings

K = Capitalisation rate.

The investors buy the shares of a company as an investment with an expectation to gain from increase in wealth of the company. They expect some return on their investment. It is the duty of the finance manager to see that the shareholders get good returns on the shares. Thus, the value of the share should increase in the stock market.

## 9.3 DISCOUNTED CASH FLOW

The discounted cash flow technique is an evaluation of the future net cash flow generated by an investment. It takes into account the interest factor as well as the return after the payback period. This method involves the following stages:

(a) Calculation of cash flows,

(b) Discounting the cash flows by of discount factor,

(c) Aggregating the discounted cash inflows and comparing them with the total discounted cash outflows.

The objective of the firm is to create wealth by using existing the future resources to produce goods and services. In order to create wealth, the discounted cash inflows must exceed the present value of cash outflows. Thus, the net present value is obtained by discounting all cash inflows and outflow attributable to be a capital investment project. For this purpose, rate of discount is chosen suitably. There are three methods of discounting cash flows, which are given below:

### (I) Net Present Value Method

Net present value method (NPV) is the most suitable method used for evaluating the capital investment projects. Under this method, cash inflows and outflow associated with each project are worked out. The present value of the cash flows is calculated by discounting the cash flows at the rate of return acceptable to the management. The rate of return is considered as a cut-off rate. It is generally determined on the basis of cost of capital suitably adjusted to allow for the risk element involved in the project. The cash outflows represent the investment and commitments of cash in the project at various points of time. The working capital is taken as a cash outflow in the initial year. The cash inflow represents the net profit after tax but before depreciation. As depreciation is non-cash expenditure, it is added back to the net profit after tax in order to determine the cash inflows. The cash inflows and outflows are discounted at a certain rate and present value of cash flows are calculated. The difference between the present value of cash inflows and present value of cash outflows is called Net Present Value (NPV). If the NPV is positive, the project is accepted and if it is negative, the project is rejected. This exercise involved in calculating the present value is called 'discounting'.

Discounted cash flow is an evaluation of the future net cash flows generated by a project. This method considers the time value of money concept and hence it is considered better for evaluation of investment proposals. If there are mutually exclusive projects, this method is more useful. Thus, the following formula is used to determine the net present value:

Net present value (NPV) = Present value of future cash inflows – Present value of cash outflows.

**Illustration 9.1:** An investment project costs ₹ 1,00,000 initially. It is expected to generate cash flow as follows:

| Year | Cash Inflows (₹) |
|---|---|
| 1 | 50,000 |
| 2 | 40,000 |
| 3 | 30,000 |
| 4 | 20,000 |

(a) What is the net present value of the project assuming a 10% risk-free rate? Should the project be accepted?

(b) If the project is risky and it is decided to use a higher rate to allow for the perceived risk. Assuming this rate is 15%, what will be the net present value of the project? Should the project be accepted?

**Solution:**

(a) Net present value at 10% discounting rate

| Year | Cash Inflows (₹) | Discounting Factor at 10% | Present Value (₹) |
|---|---|---|---|
| 1 | 50,000 | 0.9091 | 45,455 |
| 2 | 40,000 | 0.8264 | 33,056 |
| 3 | 30,000 | 0.7513 | 22,539 |
| 4 | 20,000 | 0.6830 | 13,660 |
| Present value of cash inflows | | | 1,14,710 |
| – Present value of cash outflows | | | 1,00,000 |
| Net present value | | | 14,710 |

The project should be accepted at risk free rate of 10% because net present value is positive.

(b) Net present value at 15% discounting rate

| Year | Cash Inflows (₹) | Discounting Factor at 15% | Present Value (₹) |
|---|---|---|---|
| 1 | 50,000 | 0.8696 | 43,480 |
| 2 | 40,000 | 0.7561 | 30,244 |
| 3 | 30,000 | 0.6575 | 19,725 |
| 4 | 20,000 | 0.5718 | 11,436 |
| Present value of cash inflows | | | 1,04,885 |
| – Present value of cash outflows | | | 1,00,000 |
| Net present value | | | 4,885 |

The project can also be accepted at 15% because net present value is positive

## (ii) Profitability Index

The net present value method uses discounted cash flows. It expresses cash flows in present rupees. The NPV of different projects can be compared. It implies that each project can be evaluated independent of others on its own merit. Sometimes we have to compare a number of projects each involving different amounts of cash inflows and outflows. If the cash flows are different and period of the project are also different and two or more projects give positive net present value, then we have to use the technique of profitability index which is as follows:

$$\text{Profitability Index} = \frac{\text{Present value of cash inflows}}{\text{Present value of cash outflows}}$$

The project is acceptable if the profitability index value is higher than 1.

**Illustration 9.2:** X Ltd. is considering purchase of a machine in replacement of an old one. Two models viz. 'modern' and 'sky' are offered at prices of ₹ 22.5 lakhs and ₹ 30 lakhs respectively. Further particulars regarding these models are given below:

| Particular | Modern | Sky |
|---|---|---|
| (i) Economic life in years | 5 | 6 |
| (ii) After tax annual cash inflows: | | |
| **Year** | **₹ lakhs** | **₹ lakhs** |
| 1 | 5.00 | 6.00 |
| 2 | 7.50 | 8.00 |
| 3 | 10.00 | 10.00 |
| 4 | 9.00 | 12.00 |
| 5 | 8.50 | 10.50 |
| 6 | – | 9.50 |
| (iii) Present value factors at 12% per annum are as follows: | | |
| **Years** | **P.V. Factor** | |
| 1 | 0.893 | |
| 2 | 0.797 | |
| 3 | 0.712 | |
| 4 | 0.636 | |
| 5 | 0.567 | |
| 6 | 0.507 | |

(a) Evaluate the two proposals.

(b) Which model would you recommended and why?

**Solution:**

(a) Calculation of Net Present Value

(₹ lakhs)

| Year | P.V. Factor | Modern | | Sky | |
|---|---|---|---|---|---|
| | | CFAT | PV | CFAT | PV |
| 1 | 0.893 | 5.00 | 4.465 | 6.00 | 5.358 |
| 2 | 0.797 | 7.50 | 5.977 | 8.00 | 6.376 |
| 3 | 0.712 | 10.00 | 7.120 | 10.00 | 7.120 |
| 4 | 0.636 | 9.00 | 5.724 | 12.00 | 7.632 |
| 5 | 0.567 | 8.50 | 5.954 | 10.50 | 5.953 |
| 6 | 0.507 | – | | 9.50 | 6.084 |
| Present value of cash inflows | | | 29.240 | | 38.523 |
| *Less*: Present value of cash outflows | | | 22.500 | | 30.000 |
| Net present value | | | 6.740 | | 8.523 |

(b) Considering net present value method, both the models have positive net present value and their initial investments are different. Hence, the decision will be based on profitability index which is calculated as follows:

| | Modern | Sky |
|---|---|---|
| Profitability index | | |
| $= \frac{PVCI}{PVCO}$ | $= \frac{29.240}{22.500}$<br>= 1.299 | $= \frac{38.523}{30.00}$<br>= 1.284 |

(c) As the profitability index of model 'Modern' is higher, it is recommended.

## (iii) Internal Rate of Return

Internal rate of return is that rate at which the sum of discounted cash inflows equals the sum of discounted cash outflows. It is the rate which discounts the cash flows to zero. This method also considers the time value of money, the initial cash flows and all future cash flows from the investment. The internal rate of return method does not use the desired rate of return but estimates the discount rate of return method does not use the desired rate of return but estimates the discount rate that makes the present value equal to the initial investment. The net present value of the investment will be zero in case of IRR. This estimated rate of return is then compared to a criterion rate of return that can be the company's desired rate of return. Thus, internal rate of return is the maximum rate of interest which a company can afford to pay on the capital invested in a project. A project would qualify to be accepted if IRR exceeds the cut-off rate. While evaluating two or more projects, a project which gives a higher internal rate of return would be preferred. The internal rate of return can be calculated by using trial and error method.

**Illustration: 9.3:** X Ltd. is currently under examination a project which will yield the following returns over a period of time:

| Year | Gross Yield (₹) |
|---|---|
| 1 | 80,000 |
| 2 | 80,000 |
| 3 | 90,000 |
| 4 | 90,000 |
| 5 | 75,000 |

Cost of machinery to be installed amounts to ₹ 2,00,000 and the machine is to be depreciated at 20% per annum at WDV basis. Income tax rate is 30%. If the average cost of raising capital is 10%, would you recommend accepting the project under the internal rate of return method?

Present value of money at rates of interest is as under:

| Year | At 10% | At 14% |
|---|---|---|
| 1 | 0.91 | 0.88 |
| 2 | 0.83 | 0.77 |
| 3 | 0.75 | 0.67 |
| 4 | 0.68 | 0.59 |
| 5 | 0.62 | 0.52 |

**Solution:**

(a) Evaluation of project under IRR method:

| Year | Gross Yield (₹) 1 | Depreciation (₹) 2 | Balance (₹) 3 | Income Tax (₹) 4 | Net Cash Inflows (₹) 5 | CFAT (2 + 5) 6 |
|---|---|---|---|---|---|---|
| 1 | 80,000 | 40,000 | 40,000 | 12,000 | 28,000 | 68,000 |
| 2 | 80,000 | 32,000 | 48,000 | 14,400 | 33,600 | 65,600 |
| 3 | 90,000 | 25,600 | 64,400 | 19,320 | 45,080 | 70,680 |
| 4 | 90,000 | 20,480 | 69,520 | 20,856 | 48,664 | 69,144 |
| 5 | 75,000 | 81,920 | 6,920 | – | 75,000 | 81,920 |

(b) Calculation of Net present value:

| Year | CFAT | D.F. @10% | D.F. @12% | P.V. @10% | P.V. @14% |
|---|---|---|---|---|---|
| 1 | 68,000 | 0.91 | 0.88 | 61,880 | 59,840 |
| 2 | 65,600 | 0.83 | 0.77 | 54,448 | 50,512 |
| 3 | 70,680 | 0.75 | 0.67 | 53,010 | 47,356 |
| 4 | 69,144 | 0.68 | 0.59 | 47,018 | 40,795 |
| 5 | 81,920 | 0.62 | 0.52 | 50,790 | 42,598 |
| | | | | 2,67,146 | 2,41,101 |

The present value of cash flows at 14% rate works out to ₹ 2,41,101. Therefore, IRR lies above 14%.

The actual IRR can be calculated as follows:

| Year | CFAT | D.F. @16% | D.F. @18% | D.F. @22% | P.V. (₹) | P.V. (₹) | P.V. (₹) |
|---|---|---|---|---|---|---|---|
| 1 | 68,000 | 0.862 | 0.847 | 0.820 | 58,616 | 57,596 | 55,760 |
| 2 | 65,600 | 0.743 | 0.718 | 0.672 | 48,741 | 47,100 | 44,083 |
| 3 | 70,680 | 0.641 | 0.609 | 0.551 | 45,305 | 43,044 | 38,945 |
| 4 | 69,144 | 0.552 | 0.516 | 0.451 | 38,167 | 32,912 | 31,184 |
| 5 | 81,920 | 0.476 | 0.437 | 0.370 | 38,994 | 35,791 | 30,310 |
| | | | | | 2,29,823 | 2,16,443 | 2,00,282 |

The Net present value at 22% discounting factor is around zero. Hence, the actual IRR is 22% As the cost of capital is 10% which is a cut-off rate, and IRR is 22%, the project is recommended.

**Illustration: 9.4:** The FFM Ltd. is in the tax bracket of 35% and discounts its cash flows at 16% in the acquisition of an asset worth ₹ 10 lakhs. It is given two offers either to acquire the asset by taking a loan @15% per annum repayable in five yearly instalements of ₹ 2,00,000 each plus interest or to lease-in the assets at yearly rentals of ₹ 3,24,000 for five years. In both the cases, the instalment is payable at the end of the year. Applicable rate of depreciation is 15% using written down value (WDV) method.

You are required to suggest the better alternative. P.V. factor at 16% are as follows:

| Year | P.V. Factor |
|---|---|
| 1 | 0.862 |
| 2 | 0.743 |
| 3 | 0.641 |
| 4 | 0.552 |
| 5 | 0.476 |

**Solution:**

(a) Present value of cash flows under buying options

| Year | Principal (₹) | Interest (₹) | Depre. (₹) | Tax (₹) | Net Cash Inflows (₹) | D.F. | D.V. (₹) |
|---|---|---|---|---|---|---|---|
| 1 | 2,00,000 | 1,50,000 | 1,50,000 | 1,05,000 | 24,500 | 0.862 | 2,11,190 |
| 2 | 2,00,000 | 1,20,000 | 1,27,500 | 86,625 | 2,33,375 | 0.743 | 1,73,398 |
| 3 | 2,00,000 | 90,000 | 1,08,375 | 69,431 | 2,20,569 | 0.641 | 1,41,385 |
| 4 | 2,00,000 | 60,000 | 92,118 | 53,241 | 2,06,759 | 0.532 | 1,14,131 |
| 5 | 2,00,000 | 30,000 | 78,301 | 37,905 | 1,92,095 | 0.476 | 91,437 |
| Present value of cash inflows | | | | | | | 7,31,541 |

(b) Present value of cash outflows in leasing option

| Year | Rental (₹) | Tax (₹) | Net Cash Outflows (₹) | D.F. | P.V. (₹) |
|---|---|---|---|---|---|
| 1 | 3,24,000 | 1,13,400 | 2,10,600 | 0.862 | 1,81,537 |
| 2 | 3,24,000 | 1,13,400 | 2,10,600 | 0.743 | 1,56,476 |
| 3 | 3,24,000 | 1,13,400 | 2,10,600 | 0.641 | 1,34,995 |
| 4 | 3,24,000 | 1,13,400 | 2,10,600 | 0.552 | 1,16,251 |
| 5 | 3,24,000 | 1,13,400 | 2,10,600 | 0.476 | 1,00,246 |
| Present value of cash outflows | | | | | 6,89,505 |

The better alternative is leasing.

## 9.4 ECONOMIC VALUE ADDED (EVA)

Any surplus generated from operating activities over and above the cost of capital is termed as "Economic Value Added". It is the new measure of corporate surplus. Thus, EVA is defined as "Excess Profit of a firm after charging cost of capital".

Economic Value added is the corporate surplus that should be shared by the employees, management and shareholders. Earning profit is not sufficient. A business entity should earn sufficient to cover its cost of capital and surplus to grow. Thus, any profit earned over and above the cost of capital is Economic Value Added. Maximisation of shareholder's wealth is linked to a basic proposition that return on capital employed is better than cost of capital. Capital employed means the long term capital, i.e., net worth plus debentures and long term borrowings. Cost of capital represents weighted average cost of capital.

The term EVA is recent origin. It is the registered trade mark of Stern Stewart & Co USA. It was postulated in the year 1990. It is a modified version of residual income concept. The recent thinking is that economic value added is the true measure of corporate performance.

## Measurement of Economic Value Added

Economic value added is just a way of measuring an operation's real profitability. EVA measurement requires a company to be more careful about resources mobilisation, resources allocation and investment decision. It effectively measures the productivity of all factors of production. EVA can be measured s follows:

$$\text{EVA} = \text{NOPAT} - (\text{TCE} \times \text{WACC})$$
$$= \text{NOPAT} - \text{Cost of Capital}$$

where

NOPAT = Net Operating Profit after Tax

TCE = Total Capital Employed

WACC = Weighted Average Cost of Capital

The net Operating Profit (NOPAT) is calculated excluding non-operating items like dividend, interest on securities invested outside the business and non-operating expenses. The total Capital Employed (TCE) is the sum of shareholders' fund as well as loan funds. However, this does not include investment made outside the business. Weighted Average Cost of Capital (WACC) is cost of debt after tax and cost of equity as measured on the basis of Capital Assets Pricing Model.

EVA is expressed in terms of rupee figure and not as a percentage. It measures the absolute rupee value of wealth created. EVA is regarded as comprehensive measure of performance. It is considered that this measure can be applied to each business segment within a company, to find out EVA contribution of each segment of the company.

## Capital Asset Pricing Model (CAPM)

For the purpose of measuring EVA, Cost of Equity is measured on the basis of capital Assets Pricing Model which is given below:

$$\text{Cost of Equity} = K_e = R_f + \beta\,(R_m - R_f)$$

where

$R_l$ = Risk free return

$R_m$ = Expected Market rate of return

$\beta$ = Risk Co-efficient of particular Company.

The concept of Economic Value Added is being increasingly used by companies as performance indicator. EVA is a strong tool for business planning. It explains clear surplus to the Company, which can be shared by different stockholders. EVA is also good for investors. The investors can determine, whether a company is worth investing. EVA effectively helps to explain the ability of a company to generate clear surplus. For valuation of goodwill and shares, a company may benchmark the EVA to spread. It has also been widely recognised that EVA linked employee compensation is the best way to set accountability towards shareholders and protecting and improving shareholders value. EVA can also be used as an indicator of value addition for issue of sweat equity.

## EVA as a Popular Performance Measure

The concept of Economic Value Added helps to measure the corporate performance and performance of business segment as well. For this purpose, all management divisions are modelled, monitored and communicated terms of added value to shareholders' investment. The concept of Economic Value Added is very important from the investor's point of view. It is a running score, which tells then how well managers are performing their primary task of creating wealth. Thus, Economic Value Added is a popular method of measuring the performance of the business units. The business units should produce enough profits to exceed the cost of capital. Economic Value Added attempts most appropriate determination of cost of capital. Capital employed within each division is measured and then operating return earned by that capital is measured. The focus point is that Economic Value Added is created when there is operating profit left after cost of capital has been deducted.

## Application of Economic Value Added

The concept of Economic Value Added is being widely used by the companies as a performance indicator. It is a better approach than the traditional profit indicator based on profit after tax (PAT) or cash flow. It explains clear surplus to the company which can be shared by different interest groups. Economic Value Added also represents a framework on which investors may determine, whether a business enterprise is worth investing. This helps to measure the corporate performance of a business segment as well. Economic Value Added seems to be a powerful tool that gets managers to deploy capital for maximum gain.

Economic Value Added is an important issue in corporate financial decision particularly in mergers and acquisitions. It effectively helps to explain the ability of a company to generate clear surplus. Economic Value Added spread of a company and Economic Value Added spread of the market leader explains the super profit. Economic Value Added is a measure of corporate surplus and it is possible to link Economic Value Added to valuation of goodwill and share. Goodwill can be assumed as the excess of Economic Value Added spread enjoyed by a company, over the benchmark company multiplied by average capital employed. Economic Value Added based employee compensation is the best way to set accountability towards shareholders and protecting and improving shareholders value. Annual Economic Value Added target should be established for each operation based upon previous year's target adjusted up and down based upon previous year's actual performance. Economic Value Added of the business unit should not be used as bonus, but bonus should be linked to Economic Value Added of the company.

## Economic Value Added Analysis in India

Economic Value Added revealed the gloomy performance of Indian companies. Many listed companies have started showing, Economic Value Added calculations in their annual reports for the benefit of the shareholders. The positive Economic Value Added performance has been shown by software, tobacco, tea, paints and automobile companies. The companies like Hindustan Unilever, Maruti Suzuki, ITC have been using the concept of Economic Value Added. The management accountants have been engaged in advising the companies on the issue of project appraisal, cost management and business restructuring. A management account is expected to successfully transform traditional management into value-based management. Economic Value Added is a new way of looking into corporate profit.

**Illustration: 9.5:** Calculate EVA from the following data for the year ended 31st March, 2013.

| | (₹) crores |
|---|---|
| Average Debt | 30 |
| Average Equity | 270 |
| Profit after tax, before exceptional items | 145 |
| Interest after taxes | 0.5 |
| Cost of Debt (Post tax) | 7.50% |
| Cost of Equity | 15.0% |

**Solution:**

(i) Calculation of Weighted Average Cost of Capital.

(₹ crore)

| Source | Amount | Cost% | Weighted Cost |
|---|---|---|---|
| Equity | 270 | 15.00 | 40.50 |
| Debt | 30 | 7.50 | 2.25 |
| | **300** | | **42.75** |

$$\text{WACC} = \frac{42.75}{300} \times 100 = 14.25\%$$

(ii) Cost of Capital Employed = 14.25% of ₹ 300 crore
= ₹ 42.75 crore

(iii) Calculation of NOPAT

| | (₹ crore) |
|---|---|
| Profit after tax, but before Exceptional items | 145.00 |
| *Add*: Interest after taxes | 0.50 |
| Net Operating Profit After Tax (NOPAT) | **145.50** |

(iv) EVA = NOPAT – Cost of Capital
= ₹ (145.50 – 42.75) crore
= ₹ 102.75 crores

**Illustration: 9.6:** Vijay Ltd. provides you the following information as on 31st March, 2013.

**Balance Sheet as on 31.3.2013**

| Liabilities | (₹ lakhs) | Assets | (₹ lakhs) |
|---|---|---|---|
| Share Capital | 1,000 | Fixed Assets | 2,250 |
| Reserve & Surplus | 1,300 | Current Assets | 750 |
| Long-term Debt | 200 | | |
| Creditors | 500 | | |
| | **3,000** | | **3,000** |

**Additional Information:**

(i) Profit before interest and taxes ₹ 2,000 lakhs.

(ii) Interest paid ₹ 30 lakhs.

(iii) Tax rate 30%

(iv) Risk free Rate 11%

(v) Long-term Market Rate = 12%

(vi) Beta ($\beta$) = 1.62

You are required to calculate the Economic Value Added.

**Solution:**

(i) Calculation of Cost of Equity:

$$K_e = R_f + \beta (R_m - R_f)$$
$$= 11 + 1.62 (12 - 11)$$
$$= 11 + 1.62$$
$$= 12.62\%$$

(ii) Calculation of Cost of Debt:

$$\text{Rate of Interest} = \frac{\text{Interest}}{\text{Debt}} \times 100$$
$$= \frac{30}{200} \times 100$$
$$= 15\%$$

(iii) Calculation of Weighted Average Cost of Capital:

| Source | Amount | Cost% | Weighted Cost |
|---|---|---|---|
| Equity | 2,300 | 12.62 | 290.26 |
| Debt | 200 | 10.50 | 21.00 |
| | **2,500** | | **311.26** |

$$\text{WACC} = \frac{311.26}{2,500} \times 100 = 12.45\%$$

(iv) NOPAT = PBIT – Interest – Tax

= ₹ 2,000 lakhs – 600 lakhs

= ₹ 1,400 lakhs

(v) EVA = NOPAT – Cost of Capital

= ₹ 1400 – 311.26 lakhs

= ₹ 1088.74 lakhs

(vi) Cost of Debt = $K_d$ – (I – t)

= 15 – 30% of 15

= 15 – 4.5

= 10.50%

**Illustration: 9.7:** Modern Industries Ltd. is engaged in textiles business. Its income statement and balance sheet are given below:

(i) Income Statement for the year ended 31.3.2013

| Particulars | (₹ lakhs) |
|---|---|
| **Sales revenue** | 12,000 |
| *Less*: Cost of Production | 9,000 |
| PBIT | 3,000 |
| *Less*: Interest on Loan | 20 |
| PBT | 2,980 |
| *Less* : Tax @30% | 894 |
| Earnings after tax | 2,086 |

(ii) Balance Sheet as on 31.3.2013

| Liabilities | (₹ lakhs) | Assets | (₹ lakhs) |
|---|---|---|---|
| Equity Share Capital (10 each) | 400 | Land & Building | 200 |
| Reserve & Surplus | 300 | Plant & Machinery | 400 |
| 10% Bank Loan | 200 | Debtors | 200 |
| Creditors | 100 | Stock | 150 |
| | | Cash & Bank | 50 |
| | **1,000** | | **1,000** |

(iii) The Company's weighted average Cost of Capital id 12%

(iv) The Company is listed on BSE and has a P/E Ratio of 6 times.

You are required to calculate (a) value of the firm (b) EVA and (c) MVA.

**Solution:**

(a) **Calculation of EPS**

Earnings after tax = ₹ 2,086 lakhs

Number of Equity Shares = 40 lakhs

$$\therefore \text{EPS} = \frac{2{,}086 \text{ lakhs}}{40 \text{ lakhs}}$$

= ₹ 52.15

**Calculation of the Market Price (MP) of the Share**

MP = EPS × P/E Ratio

MP = 52.15 × 6

= ₹ 312.90

**Calculation of Value of the firm**

= Market Price × Number of Shares

= ₹ 312.90 × 40 lakhs

= ₹ 12,516 lakhs

**(b) Calculation of EVA**

EVA = NOPAT – Cost of Capital

NOPAT = PBIT (1 – t)

= 3,000 (1 – 0.3)

= ₹ 2,100 lakhs

∴ EVA = 2,100 lakhs – (12% of Equity & Reserve Surplus + Bank Loan)

∴ EVA = ₹ 2,100 lakhs – 12% of (900 lakhs)

= ₹ 2,100 – 108 lakhs

= ₹ 1,992 lakhs

**(c) Calculation of Market Value Added (MVA)**

| **Particulars** | **(₹)** |
|---|---|
| Market Value of Equity Shares | 312.90 |
| Number of Equity Shares Outstanding | 40 lakhs |
| ∴ Total Market Value of the firm | 12,516 lakhs |
| *Less*: Long-term liquidities<br>(Equity Capital + Reserve & Surplus + Long-term Loans) =<br>(400 + 300 + 200) | 900 lakhs |
| MVA | 11,616 lakhs |

## 9.5 FREE CASH FLOW

A company's value depends on its free cash flow (FCF) which is defined as follows:

FCF = Net operating profit after tax – Net investments in operating capital

= NOPAT – Net investment in operating capital

= [EBIT × (1 – t)] – (Capital of current year – capital of previous year)

In a company can reduce its inventories, its cash holding or its receivable, then its net investment in operating capital will go down. If these actions do not harm operating profit then free cash flows will increase, which will lead to a higher stock price.

### Cash Conversion Cycle

Companies typically follow a cycle in which they purchase inventory, sell goods on credit and then collect accounts receivables. This cycle is referred to as the cash conversion cycle. Sound working capital policy is designed to minimise the time between cash expenditure on materials and the collection of cash on sales.

The cash conversion cycle model which focuses on the length of time between the payments made by the company and receipt of cash.

1. **Inventory conversion period:** inventory conversion period is the average time required to convert materials into finished goods and then to sell those goods. The inventory conversion period is calculated as follows:

$$\text{Inventory conversion period} = \frac{\text{Inventory}}{\text{Sales per day}}$$

For example, average inventory of a company is ₹ 2,00,000 and sales are ₹ 10,00,000, then the inventory conversion period will be 72 days as follows:

$$\text{Inventory conversion period} = \frac{2,00,000}{10,00,000 \div 360}$$

$$= 72 \text{ days}$$

Thus, it takes an average of 72 days to convert materials into finished goods and to sell these goods.

2. **Receivables collection period:** Receivables collection period is the average length of time required to convert the company's receivables into cash that is to collect cash following a sale. It is also called as days sales outstanding (DSO). It is calculated as follows:

$$\text{Receivables collection period} = \frac{\text{Receivables}}{\text{Credit sales} \div 360}$$

For example, if receivables of a company are ₹ 66,667 and sales are ₹ 10,00,000,. the receivables collection period will be 24 days as follows:

$$\text{Receivables collection period} = \frac{66,667}{10,00,000 \div 360}$$

$$= 24 \text{ days}$$

Thus, it takes 24 days after a sale to convert the receivables into cash.

3. **Payables deferred period:** Payables deferred period is the average length of time between the purchase of materials and payments of cash for them. It is calculated as follows:

$$\text{Payables deferred period} = \frac{\text{Payables}}{\text{Purchases per day}}$$

For example, if a company on an average has 30 days to pay for materials, if its cost of goods sold is ₹ 8,00,000 per year and its accounts payable average ₹ 66,667, then its payables deferred period will be 30 days as follows:

$$\text{Payables deferred period} = \frac{66,667}{8,00,000 \div 360}$$

$$= 30 \text{ days}$$

Thus, the calculated figure is consistent with the stated figure of 30 days payment period. Hence, the company has been working efficiently.

4. **Cash conversion cycle:** The cash conversion cycle nets out the three periods and equals the length of time between the firm's actual cash expenditure and its own cash receipts. Thus, the cash conversion cycle equals the average length of time a rupee is tied up in current assets. The cash conversion cycle can be expressed as follows:

$$\text{Cash conversion cycle} = \text{Inventory conversion period} + \text{Receivables collection period} - \text{Payables deferred period}$$

For example, A Ltd. takes an average of 72 days to convert raw materials into finished goods and then to sell then and another 24 days to collect its receivables. However, 30 days normally elapse between receipt of raw materials and payment for them. Thus, the cash conversion cycle will be 66 days as follows:

$$\text{Cash conversion cycle} = 72 \text{ days} + 24 \text{ days} - 30 \text{ days} = 66 \text{ days}$$

It can also be calculated in other way as under:

Cash inflow delay – cash payment delay = 72 days + 24 days – 30 days = 66 days

Free Cash Flow is a measure of financial performance calculated as operating cash flow minus capital expenditures. Free cash flow (FCF) represents the cash that a company is able to generate after laying out the money required to maintain or expand its asset base. Free cash flow is important because it allows a company to pursue opportunities that enhance shareholder value. Without cash, it is tough to develop new products, make acquisition, pay dividends and reduce debt, FCF is calculated as:

Net Income
+ Amortization/Depreciation
– Changes in Working Capital
– Capital Expenditures
**= Free Cash Flow**

In corporate finance, free cash flow (FCF) is cash flow available for distribution among all the securities holders of an organisation. They include equity holders, debt holders, preferred stock holders, convertible security holders, and so on.

| Element | Data Source |
|---|---|
| Net Income | Current Income Statement. |
| + Depreciation/Amortization | Current Income Statement. |
| – Changes in Working Capital | Prior and Current Balance Sheets: Current Assets and Current Liabilities. |
| – Capital expenditure | Prior & Current Balance Sheets: Property, Plant and Equipment Accounts. |
| **= Free Cash Flow** | |

| Element | Data Source |
|---|---|
| Net Income | Current Income Statement. |
| + Depreciation / Amortization | Current Income Statement. |
| – Changes in working Capital | Prior and Current Balance Sheets: Current Assets and Current Liabilities. |
| **= Cash Flow Operations** | Same as Statement of Cash Flows. |

Therefore,

| Element | Data Source |
|---|---|
| Cash Flows from Operations | Statement of Cash Flows. |
| – Capital Expenditure | Statement of Cash Flows. |
| **= Free Cash Flow** | |

There are two differences between Net Income and Free Cash Flow that should be noted. The first is the accounting for the consumption of capital goods. The Net Income measure uses depreciation, while the Free Cash Flow measure uses last period's net capital purchases.

| Measurement Type | Component | Advantage | Disadvantage |
|---|---|---|---|
| Free Cash Flow | Prior period net investment spending | Spending is in current dollars | Capital investments at the discretion of management, so spending may be sporadic. |
| Net Income | Depreciation charge | Charges are smoothed, related to cumulative prior purchases | Allowing for typical 2% inflation per year, equipment purchased 10 years ago for ₹ 100 would now cost about ₹ 122. With 10 year straight line depreciation the old machine would have an annual depreciation of ₹ 10 but the new, identical machine would have depreciation of ₹ 12.2, or 22% more. |

The second difference is that the free Cash Flow measurement deducts increase in net working capital, where as the net income approach does not. Normally, in a growing company with a 30 day collection period for receivables, a 30 day payment period for purchases, and a weekly payroll, it will require more and more working capital to finance the labour and profit components embedded in the growing receivables balance. The net income measure essentially says, "You can take that cash home" because you would still have same productive capacity as you started with. The Free Cash Flow measurement, however, would say, "You can't take that home" because you would cramp the enterprise from operating itself forward from there.

Likewise when a company has negative sales growth it is likely to diminish its capital spending dramatically. Receivables, provided they are being timely collected, will also ratchet down. All this "deceleration" will show up as addition to Free Cash Flow. However, over the longer term, decelerating sales trends will eventually catch up.

Net Free Cash Flow definition should also allow for cash available to pay off the company's short term debt. It should also take into account any dividends that the company means to pay.

**Net Free Cash Flow = Operating Cash Flow – Capital Expenses to keep current level of operation – dividend – Current Portion of long term debt – Depreciation**

Here Capital Expenditure definition should not include additional investment on new equipment. However, maintenance cost can be added.

**Dividends:** This will be bases dividend that the company intends to distribute to its share holders.

**Current portion of long term debt:** This will be minimum debt that the company needs to pay in order to create no defaults.

**Depreciation:** This should be taken out since this will account for future investment for replacing the current PPE. (Property, Plant and Equipment)

If the net Income category includes the income from discontinued operation and extraordinary income, make sure it is not the part of Free Cash Flow.

Net of all the above give Free Cash available to be reinvested on operation without having to take more debt.

## 9.6 RETURN ON INVESTMENT (ROI)

Return on investment is a percentage of return on the total capital employed in the business. It is also referred as return on capital employed. It provides an easily calculated and acceptable measure of economic performance of the business. It is calculated as follows:

$$ROI = \frac{\text{Operating Profit}}{\text{Capital Employed}} \times 100$$

The term capital employed is generally used in the following way:

Capital employed = (share capital + Reserve surplus + long term loans)
– (Fictitious assets and non-business assets)

The term operating profit means profit before interest and taxes. The term interest means interest on long-term borrowings. Interest on short term borrowing is deducted for computing operating profit. Non-trading incomes such as interest on Government securities or non-trading losses or expenses such as loss on account of fire is excluded.

Return on capital employed is the end-result of two forces i.e. profit margin and the turnover of capital. The profit margin is the balance of sales over cost and expenses. The profit margin provides a measure of relationship between selling price and cost and is expressed as a percentage to sales. The turnover of capital shows the relationship between sales and capital employed. It measures how effectively the resources are put to use. Return on investment is an important means of measuring management success in profitably investing in company's assets. It is very much used in investment decision making.

The concept of return on investment can be illustrated as follows:

**Illustration 9.8:** The following details are given regarding A Ltd. for the three years.

| | **(₹ lakhs)** | | |
|---|---|---|---|
| **Particulars** | **2006-07** | **2007-08** | **2008-09** |
| Sales | 60 | 63 | 65 |
| Cost | 54 | 56 | 58 |
| Profit | 06 | 07 | 07 |
| Capital | 40 | 44 | 45 |

Calculate:

(a) Return on sales.

(b) Capital turnover.

(c) Return on Investment.

**Solution:**

| Particulars | 2006-07 | 2007-08 | 2008-09 |
|---|---|---|---|
| (a) Return on Sales $= \frac{\text{Profit}}{\text{Sales}} \times 100$ | $= \frac{6}{60} \times 100$ <br> $= 10\%$ | $= \frac{07}{63} \times 100$ <br> $= 11.11\%$ | $= \frac{07}{65} \times 100$ <br> $= 10.77\%$ |
| (b) Capital Turnover $= \frac{\text{Sales}}{\text{Capital Employed}}$ | $= \frac{60}{40}$ <br> $= 1.5$ times | $= \frac{63}{44}$ <br> $= 1.43$ times | $= \frac{65}{45}$ <br> $= 1.44$ times |
| (c) ROI $= \frac{\text{Profit}}{\text{Capital Employed}} \times 100$ | $= \frac{6}{40} \times 100$ <br> $= 15\%$ | $= \frac{7}{44} \times 100$ <br> $= 15.90\%$ | $= \frac{7}{45} \times 100$ <br> $= 15.56\%$ |

The return on investment was 15%, 15.90% and 15.56% respectively for the last 3 years. The ROI in the second year was higher as compared to the first and third year.

**Illustration 9.9:** MNO Ltd. has two divisions: A and B. Return on Investments for both divisions is 15%. Details are given below:

| Particulars | Division A (₹) | Division B (₹) |
|---|---|---|
| Divisional Sales | 80 crore | 192 crore |
| Divisional Investment | 40 crore | 64 crore |
| Profit | 6 crore | 9.60 crore |

Analyze and comment on divisional performance of each with respect to Operational Excellence and Marketing Effectiveness.

***(M.U., MMS, Nov. 2010)***

**Solution:**

| Particulars | Division A | Division B |
|---|---|---|
| (a) Return on Sales $= \frac{\text{Profit}}{\text{Sales}} \times 100$ | $= \frac{6}{80} \times 100$ <br> $= 7.5\%$ | $= \frac{9.60}{192} \times 100$ <br> $= 5\%$ |
| (b) Return on Investment $= \frac{\text{Profit}}{\text{Capital Employed}} \times 100$ | $= \frac{6}{40} \times 100$ <br> $= 15\%$ | $= \frac{9.60}{64} \times 100$ <br> $= 15\%$ |
| (c) Capital Turnover $= \frac{\text{Sales}}{\text{Capital Employed}}$ | $= \frac{80}{40}$ <br> $= 2$ times | $= \frac{192}{64}$ <br> $= 3$ times |

**(i) Operational excellence:** Return on sales of Division 'A' is higher than Division 'B': Hence, Division 'A' has been operating very well.

**(ii) Marketing excellence:** Division 'B' has higher sales than Division 'A' and capital turnover of Division 'B' is also higher than Division 'A'. Hence, marketing excellence of Division 'B' is better than Division 'A'.

## Uses of ROI

The return on investment can be used for the following purposes:

(i) To measure the operating performance of an organisation.

(ii) To evaluate and control the capital expenditure projects.

(iii) To make profit-planning.

(iv) To analyse the profit by operating divisions.

(v) To analyse the profit by product-line.

(vi) Pricing of new products.

(vii) To analyse major cost areas in a cost reduction programme.

(viii) To determine the relative profitability of different projects.

## Importance of ROI

The rate of return on investment earned by an organisation should be sufficient to provide a fair return to the shareholders because they undertake the risk of employment of capital in the business. It is also required for expansion of business under conditions of general economic growth. The ROI is also required for attracting new capital whenever required and satisfy the employees and creditors for continued existence of the company. In case of inflation the real capital should remain intact and hence there should be sufficient return on investment to maintain the capital intact with adequate reserves.

An organisation should make coordinated efforts to improve the return on investment by the different departments of an organisation. The following measures should be used to improve the return on investment:

(a) By increasing sales

(b) By reducing costs

(c) By reducing capital employed

(d) By increasing profit

(e) By optimising the product mix

(f) By maximising the capacity utilisation

There are alternative ways to improve the performance of an organisation. The management has to make efforts to reduce expenses without reducing the sales or try to boost sales without increasing related expenses in proportion. Another alternative is to increase in capital turnover rate by reducing the investment. However, this is less popular alternative. There is an optimal level of investment in the assets. Too much of capital investment is wasteful but having too little may also hurt the credit standing and ability to complete. Return on investment has been widely accepted as a measure of business efficiency and therefore, constant efforts should be made for its improvement.

**Illustration 9.10:** From the following figures extracted from the Income Statement and Balance Sheet of Amar Sales Ltd., calculate the return on investment:

| | (₹ lakhs) |
|---|---|
| Fixed Assets | 450 |
| Current Assets | 150 |
| Investment in Government Securities | 100 |
| Sales | 500 |
| Cost of goods sold | 295 |
| **Share Capital:** | |
| 10% Preference Capital | 100 |
| Equity Share Capital (₹ 10) | 200 |
| Reserve and Surplus | 100 |
| 15% Debentures | 100 |
| Income from Investments | 10 |

Provision for tax @30% of net profits.

**Solution:**

It is better to prepare Profit and Loss Account and Balance Sheet of the company before computation of Return an Investment.

**Amar Sales Ltd.**

(i) Profit and Loss Account for the year ended ________

| | (₹ lakhs) | | (₹ lakhs) |
|---|---|---|---|
| To Cost of goods sold | 295 | By Sales | 500 |
| To Interest on debenture | 15 | By Income from investment | 10 |
| To Provision for tax | 60 | | |
| To Net Profit | 140 | | |
| | **510** | | **510** |

(ii) Balance Sheet as on ________

| Liabilities | (₹ lakhs) | Assets | (₹ lakhs) |
|---|---|---|---|
| **Share Capital:** | | Fixed Assets | 450 |
| 10% Preference share capital | 100 | Investment in Government Securities | 100 |
| Equity share capital | 200 | Current Assets | 150 |
| Reserve and Surplus | 100 | | |
| 15% Debentures | 100 | | |
| Profit and Loss A/c | 140 | | |
| Provision for tax | 60 | | |
| | **700** | | **700** |

(iii) Return on Investment (ROI) = $\frac{\text{PBIT}}{\text{Capital Employed}} \times 100$

$= \frac{205}{540} \times 100$

$= 37.96\%$

(iv) Net Operating Profit:

| | (₹ lakhs) |
|---|---|
| Net Profit | 140 |
| *Add*: Provision for tax | 60 |
| *Add*: Interest on debenture | 15 |
| *Less*: Income from investment | 10 |
| Net Operating Profit | **205** |

(v) Capital Employed:

| | (₹ lakhs) |
|---|---|
| Preference Capital | 100 |
| Equity Share Capital | 200 |
| *Add*: Reserve and Surplus | 100 |
| *Add*: Profit and Loss A/c | 140 |
| *Add*: Debentures | 100 |
| | **640** |
| *Less*: Investment in Government-Securities | 100 |
| Capital Employed | **540** |

## Limitations of ROI

ROI is a very important measure for judging the overall financial performance of a firm. However, there are certain limitations of the concept of return on investment which are as follows:

1. **Manipulation:** ROI is based on earnings and investments. These figures can be manipulated by the management. There are chances of manipulation in case of valuation of inventory, fixed assets, provisions, etc.
2. **Different bases for computation:** There are different bases for calculating profit and investment. The capital employed as well as operating profit can be calculated on the basis of different alternatives.
3. **Emphasis on short-term profits:** ROI emphasis on the short-term profits. This can be achieved by cutting down the costs in the short run but such cutting down of costs without justification may adversely affect the profitability of the firm in the long run.
4. **Poor measure:** ROI is a poor measure of a firm's performance because it is also affected by many external factors which are not controllable by the firm.
5. **Allocation of resources:** If there are number of divisions in a firm, there is a problem of allocation of resources. The efficiency of a department depends upon the costs and capital invested. It is difficult to allocate the costs as well as capital of each division.

On the basis of these limitations, it can be said that ROI is not an adequate measure for judging the financial performance of a business firm. However, the user must use his skill to analyse trends, compare results and note the changing patterns to devise other ratios and standards to measure more precisely the efficiency in different sectors of the business and for different classes of capital.

## ROI and EVA

Return on investment is the ratio of profit after tax to gross investment. The amount of assets employed corresponds to the sum of all assets less current liabilities appearing in the balance sheet of a company. On the other hand, economic value added is an absolute amount stated in monetary terms. It is derived by deducting from the net operating profit a capital charge. The capital charge is arrived at by multiplying the amount of assets employed by a specific rate. The relationship between ROI and EVA can be better known form the following example:

**Illustration 9.11:** The Profit and Loss account of X Ltd. for the year ended 31st December, 2009 and the Balance Sheet as on that date are given below:

(a) Profit and Loss Account for the year ended 31.12.2012

| **Particulars** | | **(₹ lakhs)** |
|---|---|---|
| Gross | | 500 |
| *Less*: Expenses | 350 | |
| Depreciation | 10 | |
| | | 360 |
| Profit before tax | | 140 |
| *Less*: Income tax @30% | | 42 |
| Profit after tax | | 98 |

The rate to be used for calculating capital charge is 10%.

(b) Balance Sheet as on 31.12.2012

| **Liabilities** | | **(₹ lakhs)** | **Assets** | | **(₹ lakhs)** |
|---|---|---|---|---|---|
| **Share Capital:** | | | **Fixed Assets:** | 500 | |
| Equity Shares of ₹ 10 each | | 200 | *Less*: Accumulated Depreciation | 200 | 300 |
| Reserve and Surplus | | 80 | **Current Assets:** | | |
| **Current Liabilities:** | | | Debtors | 100 | |
| Creditors | 150 | | Stock | 150 | |
| Bills Payable | 50 | | Cash and Bank | 50 | 300 |
| Other Liabilities | 120 | 320 | | | |
| | | **600** | | | **600** |

You are required to calculate (a) Return on investment and (b) Economic value added and comment on the relation between them.

**Solution:**

(a) Return on Investment (ROI) = $\frac{\text{Operating Profit}}{\text{Capital Employed}} \times 100$

$= \frac{140}{280} \times 100$

$= 50\%$

(b) Economic Value Added = NOPAT – Capital charge

= 98 – 10% of 280 lakhs

= 98 – 28

= ₹ 70 lakhs.

Economic value added is an absolute amount. It is stated in monetary terms. It is derived by deducting from the net operating profit, a capital charge. The capital charge is derived by multiplying the value of assets employed by a rate. Thus, economic value added is preferred to return on investment due to the following reason:

1. The overall profit of an investment centre may fall owing to decisions that increase its ROI. Where an investment centre has a ROI of 20%, it is possible for the manager to increase its overall ROI by selling an asset whose ROI is 15%. In case the cost of capital invested in the investment centre is below 15%, there would be decrease of capital costs.
2. The use of separate rates of interest for different types of assets is another advantage accruing from the use of EVA. A high interest rate may be used for investments in fixed assets and a low rate may be used for current assets. In order to consider the various degrees of risk, different rates may be used for different types of fixed assets. Thus, consistency can be established between, the measurement system and the decision rules governing the acquisition of the assets.
3. In respect of comparable investments, all investment centres have the same profit objective. However, under the ROI method, different incentives are provided for investments across business units. Where an investment centre is earning a ROI of 20%, it would be unwilling to go in for expansion unless it is in position to earn a ROI of 20% or more on additional investments expected to be made. In USA, 78% of the companies use investment centres. However, 64% of the firms use ROI for the purpose of evaluation. In India, 70% of the companies use investment centres while 92% use ROI method.

**Illustration 9.12:** You are given the following details regarding Swam Sidhi Ltd.:

**(₹ lakhs)**

| Investment Centre | Cash and Bank Balance | Inventories | Debtors/ Receivables | Fixed Assets | Budgeted Profit |
|---|---|---|---|---|---|
| A | 20 | 40 | 60 | 180 | 60 |
| B | 30 | 30 | 50 | 130 | 25 |
| C | 10 | 20 | 40 | 100 | 17 |

The corporate cost of capital relating to money invested in receivables and debtors is 7% post tax. The rate of return required by the company for investing in fixed assets is 8% post tax. Calculate the ROI and EVA from the above and show the difference between the two methods of investment centre evaluation.

**Solution:**

(a) Computation of Return on Investment:

(₹ lakhs)

| Investment Centre | Cash Bank | Inventories | Debtors | Fixed Assets | Total Investments | Budget Profit | ROI % |
|---|---|---|---|---|---|---|---|
| A | 20 | 40 | 60 | 180 | 300 | 60 | 20 |
| B | 30 | 30 | 50 | 130 | 240 | 25 | 10.41 |
| C | 10 | 20 | 40 | 100 | 170 | 17 | 10 |

A $\text{ROI} = \frac{\text{Budgeted Profit}}{\text{Total Investment}} \times 100$

$= \frac{60}{300} \times 100$

$= 20\%$

B $\text{ROI} = \frac{25}{240} \times 100$

$= 10.41\%$

C $\text{ROI} = \frac{17}{170} \times 100$

$= 10\%$

(b) Computation of Economic Value Added:

(₹ lakhs)

| Investment Centre | Budgeted Profit | Current Assets | Cost of Capital | Required Earnings | Fixed Assets | Required Return | Required Earnings | EVA |
|---|---|---|---|---|---|---|---|---|
| A | 60 | 120 | 7 | 8.4 | 180 | 8 | 14.4 | 37.2 |
| B | 25 | 110 | 7 | 7.7 | 130 | 8 | 10.4 | 6.9 |
| C | 17 | 70 | 7 | 4.9 | 100 | 8 | 8.0 | 4.1 |

$$\text{EVA} = (\text{Budgeted Profit}) - \left(\begin{array}{c}\text{Required Earnings}\\ \text{on Current Assets}\end{array} + \begin{array}{c}\text{Required Earnings}\\ \text{on Fixed Assets}\end{array}\right)$$

A = (60) – (8.4 + 14.4) = 60 – 23.8 = ₹ 37.2 lakhs

B = (25) – (7.7 + 10.4) = 25 – 18.1 = ₹ 6.9 lakhs

C = (17) – (4.9 + 8.0) = 17 – 12.9 = ₹ 4.1 lakhs

There is no consistency between the ROI objective and corporate cut-off rate in any of the investment centres. Similarly, there is no consistency with the objective and corporate carrying cot of current assets. Thus, it is worthwhile to note that if any investment centre earns more than 8% and 7% respectively or additional investments in fixed assets and current assets, its EVA will increase.

**Illustration 9.13:** From the following information of HK Ltd. calculate the ROI and EVA:

(₹ lakhs)

| Business Unit | Cash | Receivables | Inventories | Fixed Assets | Budgeted Profit |
|---|---|---|---|---|---|
| A | 10 | 20 | 30 | 60 | 24 |
| B | 20 | 20 | 30 | 50 | 14 |
| C | 15 | 40 | 40 | 10 | 10 |
| D | 05 | 10 | 20 | 40 | 04 |
| E | 10 | 05 | 10 | 10 | –02 |

Assume that the company's required rate of return of investing in fixed assets is 10% after taxes and on working capital is 4%.

Comment on the difference between ROI and EVA.

**Solution:**

(a) Calculation of ROI:

(₹ lakhs)

| Unit | Cash | Receivables | Inventories | Fixed Asset | Total Investment | Budgeted Profit | ROI % |
|---|---|---|---|---|---|---|---|
| A | 10 | 20 | 30 | 60 | 120 | 24 | 20 |
| B | 20 | 20 | 30 | 50 | 120 | 14 | 12 |
| C | 15 | 40 | 40 | 10 | 105 | 10 | 10 |
| D | 05 | 10 | 20 | 40 | 75 | 04 | 05 |
| E | 10 | 05 | 10 | 10 | 35 | –02 | –06 |

$$\text{ROI} = \frac{\text{Budgeted Profit}}{\text{Investment}} \times 100$$

$$A = \left(\frac{24}{120}\right) \times 100 = 20\%$$

$$B = \left(\frac{14}{120}\right) \times 100 = 12\%$$

$$C = \left(\frac{10}{105}\right) \times 100 = 10\%$$

$$D = \left(\frac{04}{75}\right) \times 100 = 05\%$$

$$E = \left(\frac{-02}{35}\right) \times 100 = -06\%$$

(b) Calculation of EVA:

(₹ lakhs)

| Unit | Profit | Current Assets | | | Fixed Assets | | | EVA |
|---|---|---|---|---|---|---|---|---|
| | | Amount | Rate % | Required Earnings | Amount | Rate % | Required Earnings | |
| A | 24 | 60 | 4 | 2.4 | 60 | 10 | 6 | 15.6 |
| B | 14 | 70 | 4 | 2.8 | 50 | 10 | 5 | 6.2 |
| C | 10 | 95 | 4 | 3.8 | 10 | 10 | 1 | 5.2 |
| D | 04 | 35 | 4 | 1.4 | 40 | 10 | 4 | –1.4 |
| E | –02 | 25 | 4 | 1.0 | 10 | 10 | 1 | –4.0 |

EVA = Operating Profit – Capital Charge

A = 24 – (2.4 + 6) = 15.6

B = 14 – (2.8 + 5) = 6.2

C = 10 – (3.8 + 1) = 5.2

D = 04 – (1.4 + 4) = –1.4

E = –02 – (1 + 1) = –4.0

The difference between ROI and EVA revealed that only in Unit 'C' is the ROI objective consistent with the companywide cut off rate.

There is no objective consistent with the companywide 4 per cent of carrying current assets. Business unit 'A' would decrease its chances of meeting its profit objective if it did not earn at least 20 per cent on added investments in either current assets or fixed assets. However, unit D and E would benefit from investments with a much lower return. If any business unit earns more than 10% on added fixed assets, it will increase its EVA. A similar result occurs for current assets. Inventory decision rule will be based on a cost of 4 per cent of financial carrying charges. Thus, the financial decision rules of the business units will be consistent with those of the company. EVA solves the problem of differing profit objectives for the same asset in different business units and the same profit objective for different assets in the same unit. The method makes it possible to incorporate in the measurement systems the same decision rules used in planning process.

## 9.7 EXERCISES

1. What is value? What is the purpose of value enhancement?
2. Explain the discounted cash flow method of valuation of business.
3. What is Economic Value Added? Is it superior to ROI?
4. What is Return on Investment? Why is it used in Business?
5. Explain the concept of Free Cash Flow.
6. Write short notes on:
   (a) Value Enhancement
   (b) Net Present Value
   (c) NOPAT
   (d) Capital Asset Pricing Model
   (e) Cash Conversion Cycle

7. The following are the Estimates of Modern Ltd.

   FCFF: ₹ 176 lakhs

   Growth Rate: 10 P.C.

   Weighted Average Cost of Capital: 14 P.C.

   You are required to find out the continuing value of Modern Ltd.

   (Answer: ₹ 4,400 lakhs)

8. The following information is available for Pfizer Ltd.

   PBDIT ₹ 180 lakhs

   Book Value of Assets ₹ 900 lakhs

   Sales ₹ 1,250 lakhs

   Based on an evaluation of several pharma companies, Companies Ajantha Biocon and Cipla have been found to be comparable to Pfizer Ltd. The financial information of these companies is as follows:

| **Particulars** | **Ajantha** | **Biocon** | **Cipla** |
|---|---|---|---|
| PBDIT | 120 | 130 | 200 |
| Book Value of Assets | 750 | 800 | 1,000 |
| Sales | 800 | 1,000 | 1,600 |
| Market Value | 1,500 | 2,400 | 3,600 |
| MV/PBDIT | 12.5 | 16 | 18 |
| MV/Book Value | 2 | 3 | 3.6 |
| MV/Sales | 1.9 | 2.4 | 2.3 |

   Considering the characteristics of the Company, the following multiples appear reasonable for Pfizer Ltd.:

   MV/PBDIT = 17

   MV/Book Value = 3

   MV/Sales = 2.2

   You are required to find out the value of Pfizer based on the average the above three estimates:

   (Answer: ₹ 2,837 lakhs)

9. Shan Ltd. has employed a total capital of ₹ 1,000 lakh, provided equally by 10 P.C. debt and 50 lakh Equity shares of ₹ 10 each. Its cost if equity is 14 P.C. and it is subject to corporate tax rate of 40%. The projected free cash flows to all investors of the firm for 5 years are given as follows:

| **Year** | **₹ lakhs** |
|---|---|
| 1 | 300 |
| 2 | 200 |
| 3 | 500 |
| 4 | 150 |
| 5 | 600 |

   The debt is repayable at the year and of 5 and interest is paid at each year end.

   You are required to compute:

   (a) Value of firm

   (b) Valuation from the perspective of equity holders.

10. From the following figures extracted from the books of Anand Ltd., Calculate the Return on Investment:

| | ₹ lakhs |
|---|---|
| Fixed Assets | 900 |
| Current Assets | 300 |
| Investment in Govt. Securities | 100 |
| Sales | 900 |
| Cost of goods sold | 450 |
| 10% Pref. share capital | 200 |
| Equity share capital | 300 |
| Reserve and Surplus | 255 |
| 15% Debentures | 100 |
| Income from Investments | 10 |
| Provision for Tax | 30% |

(Answer: 42.19%)

11. Mahesh Ltd. is engaged in textiles business. Its Income Statement and Balance Sheet are given below:

**Income Statement for the year ended 31.3.12**

| | ₹ lakhs |
|---|---|
| Sales revenue | 12,000 |
| *Less*: Cost of production | 9,000 |
| EBIT | 3,000 |
| *Less*: Interest on loan | 20 |
| EBT | 2,980 |
| *Less*: Tax @30% | 894 |
| Profit after tax | 2,086 |

**Balance Sheet as on 31.3.2012**

| Liabilities | ₹ lakhs | Assets | ₹ lakhs |
|---|---|---|---|
| Equity Share Capital | 400 | Land – Bldg. | 200 |
| Res. and Surplus | 300 | Plant and Mach. | 400 |
| 10% Term Loan | 200 | Debtors | 200 |
| Creditors | 100 | Stock | 150 |
| | | Cash Bank | 50 |
| | **1,000** | | **1,000** |

The company's weighted average cost of capital is 12%. The company is listed on BSE and has a P/E Ratio of 6 times.

You are required to calculate:

(a) Value of the Firm

(b) Economic Value Added

(c) Market Value Added

(Answer: ₹ 12,516 lakhs, 1,478 lakhs and 11,816 lakhs)

❖ ❖ ❖